My Black Friend Says...

Lessons in Equity, Inclusion, and Cultural Competency

by Heather Fleming

ISBN: 9781798296493
ASIN: B07P6YHD5S

This book is dedicated to the women who have helped me become:

Sandra Saunders
Fortune Russell
Willie Mae Waters
Marion Tharpe
Bessie M. Greene
Staci Porter

This book is for my husband Jimmel, my children Jordan, Jalen, and Rion, and my bonus children Kennedy and Sergio

Table of Contents

My Black Friend Says...

When I first mentioned to acquaintances in one of my online groups that I was thinking of writing a book, my friend Erin B. jokingly stated, "Please call your book 'My Black Friend,' so every white person can say, 'well, my black friend says...' and sound progressive." At first, I laughed the title off. I had somewhat settled on calling my book "Pro-Tips" or something like that, so that it would sound professional, but the more I thought of Erin's jest, the more dissatisfied with my original title I became. I mean, it was just so...blah. As I began writing, the cleverness of her title continued to grow on me for a number of reasons: it was funny, it upended the usual connotations of the phrase, and it allowed for my book to be easily quotable. The more I played with it, the more it just felt right, especially when I consider the tone I hope to set and the goals I hope to accomplish.

The irony of the title is found in the fact that the phrase "my black friend says..." usually leads to a statement that is the antithesis of what I hope this book to be. My hope is that my book will teach people how to engage in conversation that invites people in instead of turning them away, as my title phrase so often does. I have written these essays with two aims: to educate and to create more educators. There is so much misinformation and misunderstanding of issues of race and diversity that we continue to find ourselves in conversations arguing about semantics instead of solutions. I wanted to write a book that would arm people with the knowledge they needed to begin having the difficult conversations that must take place if we are ever to move forward. My other goal is that by doing this, I will create people who are capable of sharing their knowledge with others who do not understand. There is a significant amount of work to be done, and we need as many people as possible who are willing and able to do their part.

In the name of transparency, I must stress not only what I hope my book to be, but also what it cannot possibly be. I cannot, and do not intend to, speak for all people of African descent in this book, or to every experience contained within the diaspora. We are not a monolith and for that reason alone, no one book could possibly address the entirety of our experiences, feelings, thoughts, or opinions. The essays within this book are based on research from experts in the field, personal research and observation, and my own experience as a black woman. I continue to read and learn because this journey to understanding demands continual learning.

I ask that you use my book as a starting point for your study. If you are confused about where to start (once you are done reading the book, that is), I have included my own personal reading list and a list of suggested study topics in the appendix. However, reading and research can never replace relationships as the best teacher. There are a lot of people in this world with "book learning, but no common sense," as the old Southern saying goes. Common sense comes from our experiences, and the ones that have the most impact are often those based in the relationships we have. What stirs our emotions more than those we experience because of those we love? Their fears become ours. Their hopes become our best wishes. Their pains become our concern and our cause.

Danielle Allen, in her essay "Toward a Connected Society," stresses the importance of relationships in the fight for equity in our society. She outlines three types of relationships we have with others that have varying levels of influence on our personal beliefs and thought processes:

- _Bonding ties_--"connections that bind kin, close friends, and social similars to one another." (generally the strongest)
- _Bridging ties_--"connect people across demographic cleavages (age, race, class, occupation, religion, and the like)."
- _Linking ties_--"the vertical connections between people at different levels of a status hierarchy, for instance, in the employment context."

Bridging ties, despite being the hardest to develop, are the key to a truly connected society. To develop a connected society, we must use our institutions, such as schools, the military, political bodies, and churches, to best develop and utilize bridging ties. These institutions have the ability to bring people from various backgrounds, ethnicities, religions, races, etc., together to connect and build relationships.

The funny thing about relationships, though, is that proximity doesn't necessarily make one open to change. Actually, nothing changes if we do not engage in meaningful interactions with those we love. This work requires vulnerability because, as shame researcher Brene Brown states in her book _Daring Greatly_, "Vulnerability is the core, the heart, the center, of meaningful human experiences" (Brown 12). Lack of vulnerability typically means that an individual is unable to build the amount of empathy necessary to do this work.

I once heard dynamic speaker, activist, and educator Amy A. Hunter talk about this work as the act of "falling in love" with your fellow man. Specifically, what would happen if we were to fall in love (platonically) with our neighbors who are different from us? I've thought about this ever since she said it. This is basically what inclusion is asking us to do. In asking a person to move from linking ties to bridging ties, I am asking you to love that person fiercely enough to see their humanity. I am asking you to acknowledge the similarities and appreciate the differences. I am asking you to accept their problems as your own and to be willing to take the steps necessary to help them address those problems because you love them and want them to be successful.

If we view this process the same way that we would a courtship, we have a clearer idea of the "how" of equity. What we did to establish the relationship we have with our spouses or partners or close friends is what we need to do to establish these bridging ties with others who are different from us.

- Meet them in an atmosphere that allows a variety of people to come together for a common purpose
- Respectfully introduce yourself
- Get to know some basic information to find similarities that connect you
- Listen attentively as they tell their story
- Spend time together
- Listen more as they tell you of their dreams, obstacles, and experiences
- Make space for them in our lives, in our families, and in our institutions
- Be willing to stand with them against anyone who would hurt them
- Start thinking in terms of "we" instead of "us" and "them"

Another change that occurs if we view it as falling in love with our fellow man is how we view the journey. We do not view it as a walk of shame toward understanding, but instead as a journey of inquisitiveness and wonderment. I cannot even begin to tell you how important this change is for me as a person of color. I too often find myself trying to comfort a white person who is upset that they did not know certain pieces of information or history and, as a result, have been complicit in perpetuating white supremacy and contributing to the oppression of people of color. However, the shame they feel has no value in this process and often results in time and energy wasted that could have been better spent on problem-solving and learning. The difficult part of this is that vulnerability's favorite dance partner is shame. Part of my responsibility is to give you tips for how to embrace the necessary level of vulnerability while rejecting the shame responses that will inevitably come with it; to help you develop shame resilience around this issue of race.

My intent with this book is definitely not to shame anyone. In fact, in my training classes, I often teach people this mantra: "No shame, no blame; it is what it is." This year, 2019, marks the 400-year anniversary of the arrival of the first stolen and enslaved Africans in America. While we have certainly made strides in the area of race and civil rights, we have far to go. The last few years have seen an uptick in hate crimes[1], an increased number of FBI-identified hate groups[2], and an increase in divisive rhetoric at the national level.

---

[1] According to the FBI's 2017 Hate Crime Statistics, there 7,175 reported incidences, up from 6,121 the previous year.
[2] As of Feb. 21, 2019, the Southern Poverty Law Center reports that there are now 1,020 documented hate groups in the United States. There were 457 in 1999.

Four hundred years after America acquired the first slave, we continue to be able to name too many "firsts" for people of African descent in America. We just celebrated the first black president's inauguration ten years ago this past January, not because African American people just now became capable of producing a leader from among our ranks, but because enough people in the majority population just now became capable of electing him. With so much work to be done, there is very little time to center shame. We need to be problem-solving for the future, and we can only do that when shame and shame reactions are removed from the conversation, and replaced with the sense of urgency and need for efficiency that this work requires.

Pro Tip:
Imagine this as a cross-country trip from New York to Los Angeles. Bringing your shame is like bringing your mattress from home with you on the trip, and every few miles, you have to stop and make sure it's still secure. It makes the journey impossibly long and delays everyone else who has joined in, as well. It's best to leave that mattress (shame) behind and experience all the new opportunities you'll find down the road. Some of those experiences will feel like a night at the Ritz Carlton; others will feel like a pallet on a forest floor. Experience. Learn. Reflect. Think. Fall in love with the journey and the people with whom you share it.

Where to Start

We've all been there. As we begin to experience life and learn more about discrimination and inequity in our society, a moment comes when we are unsure where to go next. We have realized that there is a lot to learn and are processing past behaviors with a sense of shame about how naive, hurtful, and insensitive we previously were. Most importantly, we are deathly afraid of making the same mistakes, so we are filled with uncertainty and helplessness. Next steps feel overwhelming as we venture into the unknown.

Yet, the next steps need not be overwhelming if you remember one important aspect of social justice: this is a marathon, not a sprint. Your goal should be to beat yesterday's time as you realize that there's a lot to learn and an urgent need to learn it quickly for the sake of the people impacted by racism, discrimination, and inequity. I recommend you start with self-assessment by asking yourself the following questions:

- Where are my biases? How did they develop? (Think about childhood experiences, ideas or prejudices you heard from family and friends, stereotypes you saw in movies or through the media, etc.)

- How have my biases impacted my decision-making, relationships, political views, etc.?

- Who is in my inner circle now? Is it diverse? How have my beliefs about others been influenced by my inner circle?

- What defense mechanisms do I use when I feel threatened by labels like "racist," "prejudiced," "xenophobic," etc.? How have those defense strategies hurt others in the past?

- How much do I care about the experiences and challenges of others who may not be like me (economically, socially, racially, religiously, etc)? How much energy am I willing to expend to learn more?

- Throughout my life, what has it meant to be a member of my race? How has "whiteness" impacted my experience?

- How much am I willing to change?

The first steps in this process are internal work - an inside job, so to speak. Personal reflection, responsibility, and accountability are essential if you are to move further along. This means putting a mirror up, looking at the ugly parts, and admitting when you've caused harm to others. It means being conscientious, measured, and careful. It especially means being willing to listen without responding, and to empathize with others.

Pro Tip: Do you not know where to start figuring out your biases, or do you want an objective assessment? Harvard University researchers have developed an assessment tool to help users evaluate their biases in a number of areas including race, gender, sexual orientation, and body type.

To access this tool, go to https://implicit.harvard.edu/implicit/ and select which assessment you would like to take. You can take as many of them as you would like. Once you receive the results, please select one and take time to reflect on what they revealed to you about your biases in that particular area.

Were your results surprising? Why or why not?

_____

_____

_____

_____

_____

_____

_____

_____

_____

_____

_____

Reflecting back on your past experiences, how do you think your biases have impacted your reactions and responses to racial stress or stress created from the discussion of other types of discrimination?

_____

_____

_____

_____

_____

_____

_____

_____

_____

_____

_____

Shame vs. Guilt

In *Daring Greatly*, Brown discusses the idea of shame versus guilt. The most important distinction she makes between the two emotions is that shame is felt as an ingrained, permanent part of one's personality ("I am bad"), while guilt is specific to a situation or behavior, and is changeable ("I did something bad"). In terms of social justice, shame is a useless, often damaging emotion. When people experience shame, they activate a number of protective mechanisms that ultimately drive disconnection, which is the exact opposite of what needs to happen. This work is all about connection, and those who give in to their shame responses leave the conversation or experience anger and frustration, but remain unchanged.

The most important aspect of shame is that it ends or prevents necessary conversations that we must have around race, ethnicity, gender, religion, etc. "Shame derives its power from being unspeakable...Shame hates having words wrapped around it" (Brown 67). During difficult discussions, shame presents itself in several ways, all of which drive individuals to disconnect from the topics and people with which they most need to engage.

> According to Dr. [Linda] Hartling, [a relational-cultural theorist and researcher], in order to deal with shame, some of us *move away* by withdrawing, hiding, silencing ourselves, and keeping secrets. Some of us *move toward* by seeking to appease and please. And some of us *move against* by trying to gain power over others, by being aggressive, and by using shame to fight shame...Yet all of these strategies move us away from connection...(Brown 78)

In difficult conversations about race, these responses to shame lead to one of three reactions we have likely all seen at one point or another:
- Shutting down by leaving the conversation once we feel discomfort, avoiding any parts of the conversation that bring discomfort or challenge,

not sharing our personal thoughts and questions, or remaining silent when the topic is introduced. (*move away*)

- Agreeing with the speaker's words (even if we don't fully understand or agree), attempting to remain neutral and noncommittal, attempting to find the "common ground" without having to take a stand one way or the other, or trying not to make anyone upset. (*move toward*)

- Denying others' experiences, refusing to listen to others, attempting to derail the conversation, introducing "whataboutisms," playing the blame game, adopting an oppositional or defiant tone or standpoint, or resorting to antagonistic language and accusations. (*move against*)

We do this in order to avoid connecting to our own pain or fragility around these issues, to avoid being vulnerable. Yet, this is exactly why we have only taken small steps as a society toward eradicating the "isms" entirely. We've developed a toxic culture that views vulnerability and empathy as weaknesses, and machismo and gentility as the most desirable traits for men and women, respectively, to have. As a result, our discussions around these issues center around the appearance we want to have instead of the truth, insight, and ideas we have to offer.

Another reason we have not been able to move forward is that most white people are so insulated against racism that many are unable to effectively deal with any race-based stress. They grow up in environments "of racial privilege [that build] white expectations for racial comfort while at the same time lowering the ability to tolerate racial stress" (DiAngleo 55). Basically, most white people lead lives that do not require them to learn about other races, discuss their own whiteness, or develop close relationships with people of color.

This insulation is partly the result of isolation. Results of the Public Religion Research Institute's 2014 American Values Survey showed that 91% of white people's friends were also white. Three-fourths of all white people had absolutely no friends of color in their social circle. Whites often self-segregate into their own neighborhoods, schools, and institutions, including churches. Dr. Martin Luther King once pointed out that "the most segregated hour in this nation is Sunday at 11 AM." So, if we are separated in almost all areas of life, how else will those in the majority population learn about the impact of whiteness on minorities if we do not remove the padding and open our minds and mouths up to these difficult conversations?

The answer is that there is no other way to do it. We cannot go around the race issue anymore and so we must go through. White people must work through "this lack of racial stamina" which researcher and author Robin DiAngelo has named white fragility. They must learn to avoid "common white responses includ[ing] anger, withdrawal, emotional incapacitation, guilt, argumentation, and cognitive dissonance (all of which reinforce the pressure...to avoid directly addressing racism)" (DiAngelo 55). With the amount of work that must be done to move us forward, we cannot allow space or time for these emotions to distract us from what we need to be doing.

Part of where you start must be with the realization that you need to replace these reactions with vulnerability and valor. Brene Brown says that "vulnerability sounds like truth and feels like courage" (Brown 37). The process of addressing race and racism must begin internally with people who are courageous enough to embrace vulnerability, speak truth, and adopt an internal assessment protocol that rejects societal expectations in favor of personal engagement. Through this process, we must learn to develop shame resiliency (steps to reject shame) and utilize guilt (the healthier emotion) as a catalyst for change. Guilt leaves us feeling that even when we've done wrong, we can do something better in the future, and presents individuals with hope and an opportunity to change.

My good friend from high school, Trey, and I were recently talking about this concept over breakfast. As we chatted about the knowledge we were gaining from our chosen professions (he's a pastor), we realized how many ways in which our work was similar. We're basically trying to teach people how to process their emotions and experiences in ways that help them arrive at their purpose in the lives and service of others. He shared a chart with me that he often references in his work. It was created from Chip Dodd's book *The Voice of the Heart*, which outlined eight major feelings. For each feeling, Dodd showed how those emotions show up as a benefit and how they can impair.

Because we want to ensure that the emotions that show up to the discussion benefit us rather than impair us, we

Feelings Chart*

Benefit	Feeling	Impairment
Names woundedness and begins healing	**Hurt**	Resentment
Values and honors what is present or missed	**Sadness**	Self-Pity
Allows us to ask for help and reach out for relationship	**Loneliness**	Apathy
Helps us practice and prepare	**Fear**	Anxiety or Rage
Helps us tell the truth, dares to hope and arouses desire	**Anger**	Depression or Perfectionism
Awakens us to humility	**Shame**	Toxic Shame, Self Rejection, Pride or Rage
Allows us to seek forgiveness	**Guilt**	Pride or Toxic Shame
Shows the fullness and richness of life	**Gladness**	Happiness or Entertainment

*chart taken from the book *The Voice of the Heart*, by Chip Dodd

have to learn to process them in healthy ways. Unfortunately, many of us have not been taught to process emotions in healthy ways. If you fall into this category, please remember these four steps to processing (McCann, "Four Steps..."):

1. <u>Mind</u>--Be mindful of what you are feeling. This requires you to be self aware and to question what you're feeling, why you are feeling it, and the impact it is having on your perceptions and reactions.

2. <u>Identify</u>--Reflect upon what is triggering your emotions and why it is causing you to be uncomfortable. Is it because you are in unfamiliar territory? Is there guilt or shame associated with what you are feeling? Does it evoke a particular experience that you do not know how to evaluate? What is most likely at the root of this emotion?

3. <u>Lean and Learn</u>--Lean into the discomfort of these emotions. THIS WORK IS GOING TO BE UNCOMFORTABLE. Any expectation that it will be easy or that it will be about what "they" have done as opposed to what you have done is unreasonable. As I said in the first chapter, sometimes this work will feel like a stay at the Ritz Carlton and sometimes it will be a pallet on the forest floor. However, to co-opt the words of Jon Stewart and change them a bit: if you are sick of being uncomfortable TALKING about race, imagine how sick minorities are of experiencing it. Learn from what you are experiencing.

4. <u>Act</u>--Respond proactively in a way that allows you to transition from the impaired aspect of an emotion. This may mean changing your initial thoughts into questions. So, instead of saying, "I feel like not all white people feel that way," instead ask "how many white people have expressed this to you?" or "what has been the impact on you when white people have done these things?" In

doing this, you create new knowledge for yourself and more acceptance for the person of color with whom you are speaking.

As a former English teacher, I (of course) tried to think of a way to utilize pneumonic devices to aid with memorizing this steps, and the only thing I could come up with was the acronym MILLA. Not bad when you consider the actress Milla Jovovich's role in *Resident Evil* and how her character was so fierce everywhere she went that the Umbrella Corporation thought it was necessary to clone her. That's what I want for each of you. I want you to MILLA (Mind, Identify, Lean and Learn, Act) those negative emotions until they disappear and we need to clone you because you are so open to discussing the needs of those around you.

The ultimate message is that your first stop on this journey is inside your own heart and mind. There are a myriad of emotions that you may feel, but only a few reactions are helpful and necessary in the process. If fear shows up, we need the outward manifestation to be practice and preparation, not anxiety and rage. Remember that people of color are searching (intentionally or not) for safe spaces that honor their experiences and allow them to be themselves. You cannot create that if you are unable to display healthy reactions to racial stress.

Pro Tip:
If you are not willing to be honest and place yourself in a position of vulnerability, you may not be ready to start. This path is filled with moments of self-realization, vulnerability, discomfort, pain, and challenge. However, if you can push through these feelings, the emotional, social, and ethical reward is worth the struggle. Please reflect on the following questions to assess where you stand in the readiness process.

When you enter into a difficult conversation about a social justice issue, what does it mean to be vulnerable? What actions do you take, what do you say, what questions do you ask yourself?

_____

_____

_____

_____

_____

_____

_____

_____

What personal barriers and experiences might hinder your ability to be vulnerable in front of others?

_____

_____

_____

_____

_____

_____

_____

_____

_____

_____

_____

_____

_____

WHAT'D I DO?

"What did I do wrong?"

This question is probably the one that I am asked the most when I do a training session or speaking engagement. A nervous individual who has listened to my presentation and perceived me as safe will seek me out in a moment of quiet and pull me to the side with a friendly greeting and request for my opinion. They will then proceed to lay out a series of events that led to a big "ouch" moment, but left them confused about what they did wrong and why they were called out for it. Unfortunately, at the time this event happened, the offender is usually too upset about the potential to be viewed as prejudiced or racist to accept feedback from the person they have offended, or they are too scared to ask clarifying questions so that they can better understand what happened and why it elicited the reactions of the other party.

The fact that this is so common is an indication that we need to be discussing race much more frequently in the institutions, classrooms, halls, and homes of America. More than that, we need to be discussing WHY something is offensive instead of just expressing our anger, disagreement, and disappointment. I need only to go into the comments section of a race-related social media story to see that too many people lack the contextual knowledge to understand the nuances of the issue at hand. As a former educator in a predominantly white school district, I know that most do not know because the full context is not widely taught. Our national standards are very much centered in the majority culture and history. African American history is often an elective course taken by a handful of students, most often African American themselves. Terms like *redlining*, *blackface*, and *Juneteenth* become an optional side note for culturally-aware teachers, but can be ignored by most, because that information will not be on the standardized tests districts and education departments use to measure teacher and school effectiveness.

The reality of our educational system is that so much information is not addressed because, as DiAngelo says, white people are insulated from racial stress. Most do not talk about race because they do not have to. When I was teaching African American History and Literature at my high school, most of my students were African Americans just like me. In those classes, we addressed a myriad of issues, but in my "regular" English courses, I was much more limited by a number of factors: choice of literature, parents, and administrators who catered to parents.

I remember one incident that occurred during the 2016 election cycle. I use the two presidential candidates to teach logical fallacies, and assigned a mini research project that asked students to look up a certain logical fallacy and how the candidates had activated that fallacy to win voters over. Unfortunately, one candidate utilized these fallacies more than the other, and by the time I finished presentations, I ended up in the grade-level principal's office for leaning heavily in one direction as opposed to the other.

I inevitably had to push back against the suggestion that I limit my discussion of politics. I was being asked to accommodate this student's need to be insulated against racial stress, and because my answer was a resounding no, a few students (with parent support) were changed out of my classes for the following semester. One of my guiding questions at that point became, "How many Jewish teachers were asked to not address Nazism in the classroom?" The reality is that asking African American teachers not to address the blatant racism and prejudice they see in our systems, both political and economic, is grossly unfair to the point of being unethical. I was not indoctrinating my students; I was asking them to care about the lives of my children, husband, family, friends, and skinfolk by asking them to think logically about the choices before them.

Limiting discourse and encapsulating people in these racially stress-free bubbles of privilege often creates a situation where people develop biased opinions and language that are damaging to others around them, even when they are not intended to be. Sometimes, people new to the social justice journey make statements that previously seemed acceptable, only to discover that they are not because they've never discussed what was wrong with the statement from another experience. I have compiled a list of common examples and written a short explanation (with contextual and/or historical perspective) of why they might be perceived as "wrong."

"I'm not racist, but..."--This phrase is often an indicator that something racist or prejudiced will, in fact, follow. Before you make this statement, consider why your phrase would need this disclaimer. People who say this before their statement often already know intuitively that it is problematic. Take the time to pause and examine why BEFORE you say it. The conversation will change for the better if the potential statement is examined as "Is my opinion based upon unconscious bias?" as opposed to "Convince me that my opinion IS racist." Again, you must remember that you are learning. Questions open conversation and invite learning.

"What about black-on-black crime?"--Research shows that most crime is committed within your immediate proximity and social group/community. The US Department of Justice's report *Race and Hispanic Origin of Victims and Offenders* , 2012-2015 states that most crime is committed intra-racially, meaning that across all races, perpetrators of crimes will be of the same race as their victims. So the term "black-on-black crime" implies that somehow African Americans are more prone to commit crimes against their fellow skin mates than members of other races are. The fact that there is no equally-used term for other races emphasizes the fetishization of African Americans as criminals, advancing a racist narrative and stereotype.

"You're so articulate!"-- A dear friend of mine (who is white) and I were having a conversation about this particular phrase, and she told me a story that I think illustrates what often happens. She is an expert in a field where excellent customer service and communication skills are absolutely essential to performing well. One day, after an African American member of her team gave a great presentation for a large group, my friend went to him and gave him feedback based on how excellent his communication and presentation skills were. She was providing him with feedback specific to their field when she told him how articulate he was. However, she instantly noticed a little change in him that made her wonder exactly what she had said that did not sit well. What was meant as a compliment was viewed as an insult, and she could not figure out why. Thank goodness, my friend had the cultural competency to be able to make that a moment of learning, connection, and adjustment, but for others, it could have had disastrous results.

Again, my friend was giving feedback specific to her field, feedback she had given white colleagues previously when they had done exceptionally well, like this young man had. However, in most situations when this phrase is uttered, it is confirmation of the speaker's unconscious bias. One is impressed by the fact that an African American is capable of of this speech, because they came into the situation prepared for the stereotypical presentation of that person.

What was intended as a compliment turns into an insult because of that person's prior experience with others uttering that phrase. Historically, white people have stated it from a condescending standpoint. When white cultural standards are used to determine what professional language sounds like and then white people express surprise that people of other cultures are capable of using it, comments like "you're so articulate" can appear as the communication of climate and expectation that is steeped in whiteness.

Unfortunately, because of what has happened in the past, the phrase has become so weighted down with these negative connotations that even individuals who don't carry those attitudes or intentions feel the backlash of using it. The best action to take is to use other terms and phrases to express the fact that you are impressed with the person because of who they are and what they can do, period. I personally prefer compliments that deal with the substance of what I say and the impact it made. So as opposed to saying, "You're so articulate," perhaps say "Your communication was very clear and easy for me to understand."

I hope I'm making myself clear. (smile)

"I can't be racist; I have black _____ (friends, family)."

At the time of the writing of this book, those interested in politics are debating over Representative Mark Meadows' comments in a House Oversight Committee hearing with President Donald Trump's former personal attorney Michael Cohen. During the hearing Meadows brought out African American HUD appointee Lynne Patton to disprove Cohen's claim that Trump was racist. When Representative Rashida Tlaib pointed this action out as racist, Meadows became incensed and stated that he cannot possibly be racist because he has nieces and nephews who are black, and he has been friends for years with the head of the committee, Representative Elijah Cummings.

I'm not here to conjecture on Rep. Meadows' stance on race, but I will say as a first introduction to this man for me...it was not good. This phrase is usually indicative of someone who understands the blatant acts of racism that occur, but not the nuances. The problem is that too often, our society has framed racism as blatant, individual acts that remove the nuanced, systemic aspects of racism. This allows people to declare "I'm not racist!" because they did not use the "n-word," while still upholding systems and practices that negatively impact minorities more than the majority.

Consider this. As our Founding Fathers fought for life, liberty, and the pursuit of happiness for all, they did so while living and depending on the labor and assistance of enslaved people, human beings that they valued as only three-fifths of a white person. Thomas Jefferson fathered at least six children with Sally Hemmings, the enslaved woman who was his wife's half-sister, while also writing this about Phillis Wheatley (and black art, in general):

"Misery is often the parent of the most affecting touches in poetry. Among the blacks is misery enough, God knows, but not poetry. Love is the peculiar oestrum of the poet. Their love is ardent, but it kindles the senses only, not the imagination. Religion, indeed, has produced a Phillis Wheatley; but it could not produce a poet."

Jefferson's positions on Phillis Wheatley and black people in general were so blatantly racist that Benjamin Banneker, brilliant architect, designer, and inventor, wrote him a letter addressing it. We could probably spend the remainder of this book providing story after story of white people who utilized the gifts and bodies of black people while still holding racist ideals about those same people.

This statement is wrong because it only speaks to proximity to people of color, not to your intentions toward them. That can only be shown through your actions.

"I don't see color/race; I'm colorblind"--When I was in the classroom, I started my semesters with an activity where I asked kids to listen to a statement I made and then move to one side of the room or the other to show if they agreed or disagreed with my statement. I always made sure that I had this one in here so that I could set the tone and expectations of discussions of race. Inevitably, it would end up being evenly split, and I would ask students on both sides why they chose the position that they did. Some kids were able to express that it was difficult for them to decide because on one hand, they always notice whether someone is of a different race or ethnicity, but on the other hand, that difference was not something they wanted to judge people for, good or bad.

First, that always showed me that I had some really smart, amazing students. Secondly, it allowed me to offer this explanation to them. I wanted them to see me. My skin color; the fact that I was a woman; the fact that I looked amazingly young for my age (wink); the fact that I was not thin. I wanted them to see me because all of those aspects partially made me who am, and have informed my experiences. What I did not want them to do is use stereotypes to form their opinions of me because of those things. By telling them this outright, I began the process of creating an environment that normalized discussions of race, ethnicity, body positivity, religion, and other demographics and guided students toward appreciation of differences, as opposed to fear.

I do not want any of my friends to be colorblind. I want them all to learn how to embrace my humanity.

"I treat everyone the same/equally."--Every first day of each new semester as an educator, I would look out at my beautiful new babies (that's what I called my students), and inform them that I was an unequal teacher. I did not treat every student the same at all. I gave some more love, others more tough love, still others even tougher love. I didn't treat them equally because they were not in my classroom under equal circumstances. Some had never been told how smart they were, while others had been convinced that they were so smart they were above criticism. Some came to class fed, so their only need was education, while others came so hungry they could not concentrate on their education. When my main goal was to provide them all with the knowledge they needed to be successful in the future, it was inherently unfair to treat them all equally.

That's what we have to consider when we say that we treat everyone the same: what does that mean in an unequal society? Is it fair to treat everyone the same when they are obviously not? My answer is no.

We must have clarity of words and thoughts as we try to express what we mean. Do you mean that you treat everyone with the same level of kindness? Do you acknowledge everyone's level of humanity equally? Do you try to make sure that everyone you encounter, regardless of identity, will feel loved and accepted? I would posit that if your answer is yes to any of those questions, you cannot possibly be treating them "the same."

The idea of treating everyone "the same" becomes problematic when that "sameness" is created according to a white, Christian, heterosexual, middle class cultural standard. People in poverty need something different than the upper middle class in order to feel accepted. People of the Islamic faith need something different than followers of Taoism or Judaism. "Sameness" only allows for one type of voice in the room. Fairness and inclusion makes room for all.

According to this standard, no one should want to be treated the same, but instead treated according to who they are and all the experience they bring.

"The same thing happens to me because I'm a _____ (woman, man, white person, etc.." --Sometimes individuals engaged in a conversation about race may try to equate their own experiences as a member of a particular demographic with that of a racial minority. The reasons they do so may range from a perfectly innocent attempt to make connection, to a more malignant attempt to deflect from the subject at hand. No matter the reason for doing so, the impact is that it feels like an attempt to negate the experiences of people in that racial minority. At a time when their voices should be heard and amplified, the minority group member may feel that they are being silenced and the voices of the majority are again being centered.

There is no equivalent experience to being a racial minority. It comes with its own unique set of issues, stereotypes, judgments, etc. The obstacles I encounter as a woman of color are patently different than white women or gay men or Muslims, and so on. We all have to get into the habit of addressing the topic at hand, and we cannot do this if we turn the conversations back to our own issues of oppression.

However, a time will necessarily come when you will need to tap into your own experience in order to be able to empathize with others. For example, you may not ever fully understand the fear I have for my sons and daughter when they leave the house without me, because there's so much additional cultural and social context to this issue when one is an African American mother. Yet, you can understand the fear you may have felt as a parent when you thought your children may be in danger, or remember your own parents staying up at night worrying about you until you arrived home safely. These experiences, and the accompanying emotions that came with them, can help you to be more sympathetic and empathetic of others' experiences. It's important that you first sit and listen to the stories and thoughts of others so that you can clearly understand what they are trying to convey. By not listening and instead trying to match oppression for oppression, one can prematurely end a conversation that would have taught you more and allowed you to clearly understand how your experience, though similar, is not equivalent.

"Well, what about...?"--When a person interjects another issue/example in an effort to negate what a person of color is saying, it is harmful to that POC and to any efforts to engage in productive conversation about this topic. For example, once during yet another training course I was required to attend for the benefit of my white colleagues, I was sharing a story about some aspect of my experience as a black woman when a white male colleague brought up something that had happened to him as an example of "reverse racism," and said that it also happens to people of other races, including white people. There was so much I could have explained about what was misleading in his statement (especially the fact that reverse racism is a myth), but I already knew that his purpose in making this statement was not to understand, but to deflect. It effectively ended that conversation and impacted our collegial relationship because that statement (along with a few other occurrences) revealed something about his thought processes and beliefs that indicated a disdain for people who look like me.

I'm not saying that you should never ask "what about...?," but it should certainly be followed by something that brings understanding, not disconnection. When you enter the conversation, question your motives for asking the question. Did you MILLA (Mind, Identify, Listen/Learn, Act) first? Is your question part of the action you are taking to respond proactively and positively? If it is not, you might want to continue listening and learning until you are prepared to move to the Act stage.

"Can I touch your hair?"--Recently, I was doing my daughter's hair and when I told her that I was going to flat-iron her hair so she could wear it straight, she became upset. She did not want to wear her hair down because the other kids at school will keep touching it. I was stunned that at 10 years of age, this was something she would have to regularly deal with. I explained to her that it was okay for her to tell her classmates that they did not have permission to touch her hair, but she said sometimes they do not ask or do not listen when she says no.

Hair seems like a fairly innocuous aspect of our shared experience. Why would it be a problem? The answer is that it mainly is problematic to ask a person of color to touch their hair because it has been used in a process of "otherization" that makes us different from the majority in every way, including our hair. It is especially problematic to touch it without permission because of the idea of consent and agency over our own bodies.

Basically, we are not pets or dolls to be touched without permission, or "other" beings to be viewed as outside of normal human experience. As shocked as I tried to be that this was my daughter's experience, I had to remember an experience I had just two years ago. I was in a meeting with an administrator, counselor, parent, and student to discuss the student's individualized education plan (IEP). I had just gotten a new hairstyle utilizing the crochet method of installation and was feeling quite fabulous with a hairstyle slightly reminiscent of Diana Ross's signature look. As I finished an awesome evaluation of the student's abilities, successes, and my ability to support the student toward greater accomplishments, I prepared to leave. When I leaned down to pick my bags up, the administrator said, "I just have to touch it," and reached out and touched my hair without my permission. I was furious and felt violated physically and professionally. I felt she, unintentionally, reduced my professionalism down to a pat on the head right there in front of these other individuals in room, all of whom were white.

This is what is called a *microaggression*, which is any action or statement directed toward a member of a marginalized group that indirectly, subtly, or unintentionally discriminates against that group. I want to stress that intent is not a determining factor in whether or not an action is discriminatory in nature. In my situation above, I know that this is not what the administrator intended to do. In fact, she is one of the nicest people I know and would never do anything to intentionally hurt anyone. Yet, intent does not matter when the impact is still the same. It is best to be intentional in understanding what a microaggression is and developing strategies for avoiding them.

"I can't pronounce your name; I'm going to call you _____ instead."--One of the best lessons I have ever witnessed in not allowing a microaggression to stand came from Quvenzhane` Wallis in 2013. She was speaking to Ryan Seacrest, who declared that he was just going to call her "Little Q," and she firmly let him know that her name was Quvenzhane`, communicating her expectation that she would determine what she would be called, not him. She was nine years old at the time.

I was so impressed by this, and upon considering it more, I realized this was absolutely the response she should have had. If we can learn collectively as a matter of cultural competency to say Michelangelo, Tchaikovsky, and Dostoevsky, we can learn Quvenzhane`. To not call a person by their name reduces their humanity and again otherizes certain groups of people. It communicates to them that we do not care enough to learn how to say just a few syllables, a name that might be common in their culture. Meanwhile, we think names like Heather are easy to say, but make fun of people whose accents do not allow them to say it properly. Does that seem fair or inclusive to you?

If you need to ask several times, that's okay. At the beginning of each semester, I would ask my students with more complicated names how to pronounce them and try to spell them out phonetically on my attendance records. As I was in the learning process, I would frequently check back in with them to make sure I was saying it correctly. I do not have empirical data to determine the impact this had, but I do have anecdotal data in the form of relationships. My room and the room of other teachers who took the time to know their names often became safe havens for these students. If the goal is to be inclusive of all people, knowing the proper pronunciation of people's names is essential. "For students, especially the children of immigrants or those who are English-language learners, a teacher who knows their name and can pronounce it correctly signals respect and marks a critical step in helping them adjust to school" (Mitchell, "Mispronouncing Students' Names..."). As an educator, I had a clear understanding of the fact that students do not learn well in environments where they do not feel respected. I also understood how unfair it was to ask students to check their identity at the door in order to "fit." I had been asked to do it too many times to count, and I did not fully thrive in these environments.

Please take time to learn people's names. It is no one's right to define other people, so if we are going to fully see a person's humanity, we must allow them to teach us about themselves. Step one is their name.

"But you're not like them..."--I grew up in a predominately white suburb of St. Louis called St. Charles. My graduating class had approximately six or so people of color in a sea of more than 300 white students.

The number of times I've heard this statement is innumerable, and often, it was preceded by something that was racially insensitive at best, blatantly racist at worst. They stated this in an attempt to separate me from the person they were using to stereotype African Americans as a whole, people worthy of the exclusionary, heavy-handed tactics being used by those in positions of power to exclude and deny.

Here's the thing of it, though. Most times, the example that these individuals were pointing to were either outliers in African American culture or people who actually just like me, but were being stereotyped or mischaracterized. Most African Americans are just like me in terms of abilities, values, goals, and dreams. The biggest way that some differ from me is in opportunity, and this difference has the most significant impact on behavior, lifestyle, and challenges.

Finding me to be the exception was another way that this person maintained their insulated view of society as a whole. This person was basically saying that it was easier to consider me the exception than to face how their biases and perceptions were inaccurate and influenced by highly-biased sources such as the media and politicians. It allowed them to not face the cognitive dissonance between their knowledge of me and their overall understanding of people that look like me.

People of color are not a monolith. We come as varied and diverse within our cultural groups as people do interculturally. Though there will always be extraordinary people throughout the world, no one should be viewed as an exception, but rather as another example of the richness that comes from diversity.

<u>"You're my spirit animal."</u>--When one goes to a search engine and enters "spirit animal," the results contain dozens of cutesy quizzes where one can determine if their personalities are more closely aligned to a wolf or turtle. That alone signifies everything wrong with using this phrase, especially in relation to other human beings. The results of this search does not center the significance of spirit animals in Native American culture nor emphasize the sacred nature of the rituals connected to assigning a spirit animal.

Native American nations place the highest value on the interconnectedness of all living beings. Many believe that

> discovering who your animal guides are is a process of paying attention to the spirits around you and following the signs. It is a process of developing your inner knowledge and spiritual understanding. An individual can not be assigned a spirit guide by another person, regardless of who that person maybe, no more than another person can say how or when the Great Mystery of Life will be known to you (Moore "Spirit Guides...")

The very idea of a spirit guide or spirit animal is something that should surely not be reduced down to an online quiz or a light joke between friends.

The other aspect of the spirit animal faux pas is naming a fellow human being as such, even if you are doing so to be respectful and express a perceived connection. Humans are not animals. This is often even more offensive to people of color who experience regular microaggressions and stereotypes that attempt to dehumanize them.

So how do you express this idea without misappropriating the Native American culture? Maybe some of the following phrases would be better:

- You're my kind.
- You're one of my people.
- "Did we just become best friends?"--iconic line from the movie *Stepbrothers*
- You're my patronus.
- You're my guardian angel.
- You're my spiritual doppelganger.

Whatever you choose, be sure to apply a similar culturally-sensitive lens to be sure you did not exchange one offense for another.

"That was savage."--Many times, it's not the dictionary definition of a word that gets you in trouble, but instead the connotations of that same word. When explaining this concept to my students, I always used the difference between *naive* and *ignorant* to illustrate what I meant. Both words mean the same thing: lacking in knowledge. However, which one would you use to describe your best friend versus the one you would use to describe the school bully?

The word *savage* becomes racially loaded, not because of its meaning, but because of the images and associations the word evokes. White colonizers used this word to describe people, particularly Native Americans, who they felt were uncivilized and culturally beneath them. As a result of their feelings toward these various cultural groups, millions were killed, enslaved, and victimized. This mentality led to The Trail of Tears, Wounded Knee, The American Indian Wars, and the eradication of whole tribes and cultural traditions. The word moved beyond adjectival descriptor to become an oppression-based moniker for entire nations of Native American people. Because of its connotation, *savage* has become a pejorative for members of our indigenous groups, and the best thing to do is to only use it in connection with something particular (i.e. the panther savagely attacked its prey), but not as a general descriptor (he/she is a savage).

Reflection: Are there any other phrases you have ever used, knew it bothered someone, but did not understand why? What was it?

Pro Tip:
There are still so many phrases that I could have added to this chapter. In fact, I probably could have dedicated this book solely to discussing just this topic. If you find yourself in a situation where you've used one of these phrases and have offended someone, it is not enough to just say that you are going to stop using it. The most important thing you need to do is find out WHY it was offensive. This will require doing some research (please use reputable, unbiased sources as often as possible) and having some difficult conversations. Be prepared for the process.

The Proper Apology

Here's a scenario for you:

You're in a conversation with a person of another experience (race, sexual orientation, ethnicity, religion, etc.), and you really want to make a connection. You know that there are topics you could (and probably should) examine with this individual, but you're concerned about offending them and losing the possibility to learn from and develop a relationship with them. You cycle through a number of things you could say but you're concerned that you may say it all wrong, so instead, you just stay quiet and miss your moment to become a true ally.

Does this sound familiar? I'm sure at some point either you or a friend has expressed anxiousness at the idea of diving into this conversation. Concern that your attempt to be an ally will end in disaster has kept you from engaging in the dialogue that we MUST have if we are ever going to solve some of the racial issues we have here in the United States and around the world. Unfortunately, I cannot offer you much comfort in this area.

You are going to make mistakes. You're going to get words wrong. You're going to speak from a place of privilege and naivete` that will disappoint and cause anger. Please know that I am not giving you permission, but presenting you with reality. It just is what it is. However, you must remember that the idea of not speaking up because you might mess up is an operation of white privilege. It puts your self-perception as a good person above the needs of people in oppressed groups to have informed allies.

If you hope to become an ally (or, even better, an accomplice) you must get used to the idea that you will not always get this right. As an African American woman, I have watched countless friends err over and over again on the issues of race, but what ended up counting the most to me was the effort they were making to become better allies and their ability to make it right once they realized their mistake.

Your greatest tool as you are building your knowledge and gaining skills as an ally will always be your ability to properly apologize when you make a mistake. Apologizing properly allows for you to learn from the mistake you made and to continue building connection with the person you have hurt or harmed. An apology contains two key elements: remorse and acknowledgment of the hurt you caused (MindTools Content Team, "How to Apologize"). I know that it is very difficult at times to put our pride aside and admit that we were wrong, but you must do it if you are going to move forward.

When a person of color or a member of an oppressed group tells you that your words and actions have hurt, trying to justify your actions will only cause further hurt and disconnection. You will waste valuable time and the potential for a deeper relationship with this person if you do so. The only correct action will be to begin the process of correcting your actions, learning from the feedback you're given, and considering how to do better in the future.

My husband and youngest son are avid sports enthusiasts, so I think about it like this. When a person first begins playing a team sport, there are plenty of mistakes made in all areas: strategically, individually, as a teammate, and as a position player. What happens when these errors are made by the most effective players and coaches on the best teams? I imagine it's similar to this:

- The whole team is on the field/court working together to defeat the opposing team (their common enemy).
- Player 1 messes up a play and accidentally hurts Player 2 in the process.
- Player 2 or Coach call a timeout and has the team gather around.
- Coach or Player 2 asks Player 1, "What just happened there?"
- Player 1 explains why they took the action they did, but acknowledges that it did not have the impact they intended.
- Player 1 may or may not understand what went wrong and why the play didn't work. Either way, Player 1 apologizes to Player 2 for hurting him, takes responsibility for what happened, and promises to be more careful in the future.
- Coach is able to explain to Player 1 what he observed and explain why it didn't work.
- The team returns to the field with new knowledge and attempt to not repeat that error again (especially Player 1).

This is very similar to the process you should go through if you ever find yourself in this position. I need to stress again that you definitely will be here eventually, because you'll begin to understand why, just like Player 1, you need to take the field with your team for every single game. You will understand that you cannot exercise the privilege of telling Coach you wish to sit some games out when you are playing against a tougher team or when you feel insecure about your abilities. Instead, you will engage the other team with the mental toughness and stamina you are building through the work you are doing off the field (reading, listening, studying, and practicing with those with more expertise).

Generally, there are at least three main parts to an apology: acknowledgement that you did something wrong or hurt someone, an expression of remorse and acceptance of responsibility, and an action step to make amends or change your behavior for the future. All of these steps are necessary if you are going to repair the hurt done by your actions, maintain your relationship with the person injured, and learn something from what happened in the process. Each step is significant for a number of reasons, and none can be missed in the process.

Acknowledgement That You Did Something Wrong or Hurt Someone

When you realize that you have said something wrong or hurt someone, intentionally or unintentionally, there will be a moment when you are brought to awareness. For some, it will be obvious, such as the person saying, "hey, what you said or did offended me." For others, the indicator may be a look, a subtle shift in body language, a withdrawal from the conversation or interaction, or another action along these lines. Once you notice, you should not hesitate to take action. First, take a second to think about what you said or did and why that person might have taken offense. If you are able to identify it, then you can say, "I now realize why that may have offended you." If you cannot directly identify it, you are perfectly correct to say, "Did something I just said offend you? That really was not my intention, and I want to understand why so that I don't make that mistake again." Either way, you have acknowledged the error and begun the process of correcting it.

An Expression of Remorse and Acceptance of Responsibility

Once you have acknowledged that you erred, it is important to express that you are sorry for your actions and that you accept responsibility for them. This is often the part where the apology goes wrong. Pride can sometimes stand in the way of saying what we need to say to repair the hurt from our words. Some of us have an almost desperate need to be viewed as good, righteous, and infallible to the point that just admitting that we were wrong, devoid of excuses, disclaimers, and projections, is nearly an impossible task.

However, it must be done in this situation. Doing so is as simple as two statements:

- I sincerely apologize for the hurt my actions caused you.

- I take full responsibility for their impact, regardless of my intentions.

Notice that there are no disavowals, no in-depth discussions of your actual views on the subjects, no pleas to be seen as a "good person." In fact, these two apology statements, made together, place emphasis instead on your understanding that *impact always trumps intent.*

Let me repeat that for you.

Impact always trumps intent. If I'm in the yard playing baseball with the kids, and I INTEND to hit a homerun, but instead hit the ball through my neighbor's window, the IMPACT of my actions will be what matters most. I cannot just go to my neighbor and say, "well, I'm good because I intended to hit it over your house into the next neighbor's backyard." Instead, I must deal with the impact of my actions. It is the same with this situation.

In fact, I would argue that in focusing upon the impact of your actions, you would have already done far more to show that you're a good person, because you are centering the other person's needs instead of selfishly making the conversation about your own perception of self and how you are perceived by others. Is that not part of what we think good people do: put others first?

An Action Step to Make Amends or Change Your Behavior for the Future

Once you have acknowledged your error, expressed remorse, and accepted responsibility for your actions, the final step is to create an action step that will allow you to SHOW your sincerity about the first few steps. A common statement that I often use is that "the best apology is changed behavior." It is simply a universal truth. An apology does not amount to much if there is not changed behavior to support it. As a result, I would argue that this is the most important portion of the apology. This is the part that will bring true healing to the relationship.

Two necessary aspects of this phase are listening and learning. You must listen to the feedback you receive from the individual you offended and take time to reflect on changes you need to make to ensure that you do not do that again. It could be as simple as not using a phrase or expression again, but that promise must be combined with understanding why the words you said were offensive so that you can develop cultural competency in the process. For example, in the previous chapter, I discussed the idea of not using "spirit animal" as a descriptor. Just agreeing to not use that phrase anymore is a simple fix, but if you gain an understanding of why it was not okay to use that phrase, you would probably understand why you also should not use "savage" as a descriptor, either, because your overall understanding will be directly tied to an appreciation of Native American culture and humanity.

Also, just agreeing to not use the phrase continues to center one's desire to maintain a positive outward appearance of advocacy. Gaining understanding leads one to place value on the other person's experience. We spend our time on what we value, so the time spent talking, researching, listening, and learning is an indication that we value those outside our experience. Realize that people outside of white, heterosexual, Christian, etc., culture have already had to spend plenty of time talking, researching, listening, and learning about those experiences as a matter of survival and success.

I would caution, though, against placing the responsibility for this phase in the lap of the person you offended. It is not that person's responsibility to determine your next actions or means of atonement. They do not have to do it, and you should not expect it of them.

I remember once that I lost a friend for just this reason. In protest of the confirmation of a political figure, a suggestion was going around the internet that women should kneel. This is post-Colin Kaepernick's expulsion from the National Football League for doing so and after a host of examples of backlash against black athletes, politicians, and citizens who supported him. I pointed out that appropriating Kaep's protest would not be a good idea and explained that it would overshadow what this particular movement represents. After requesting that my friends not participate in anything like that, one woman that I was developing a budding friendship with basically demanded that I tell her what she should do instead. When some of my white allies pointed out that this was not my responsibility and tried to talk to her about why, she became enraged and struck out against me and my friends. She eventually unfriended me once I offered her my honest opinion and agreed with my other white allies.

This woman made it through the acknowledgment step semi-well, went downhill during the remorse and acceptance step, then totally imploded while trying to make amends. The result was that I lost a potential future ally because I would not do her work for her.

The sad part was that I really liked her. That is the reason why I took time to try to explain it to her. I was giving her my time to show that I valued her. She just did not value me as much. That becomes another aspect of this journey to understand: a person from an oppressed group owes you absolutely none of their time, attention, respect, admiration, intellectual or emotional energy, or reasoning. If a person of an oppressed group takes time to explain something to you, it is because you mean something to them. However, this is purely voluntary. If they choose not to, you must accept this and find another way to learn and make a connection. To demand any of those things from that person is another operation of white privilege that must be viewed through one's personal biases.

Ultimately, the responsibility for making amends and behavioral changes lies within the person who committed the offense. Whatever change you decide to make, though, please remember that "your apology needs to be as loud as your disrespect" (as the saying goes). Your level of atonement should be equal to your level of offense in terms of gravity and scope. If your offense was committed via group email, your apology should be stated both to the person individually, as well as via group email to the same individuals who witnessed your initial offense.

The purpose of this is not to embarrass or humiliate you. You must think in terms of the repercussions that the other person may suffer in terms of professional standing, personal humiliation and embarrassment, relationships with their colleagues, and perceptions by supervisors and managers as a result of your action.   A prime example of this happened to me in my first couple of years of teaching. My birthday is on Halloween, and a well-meaning colleague sent a message out asking my department and administrators to say happy birthday to their favorite "spook." She did not know that this word was a pejorative that had been used to denigrate African Americans, because she came from a small town where she had been insulated against discussions of race. When she came to me to apologize, I asked her to send an email out with her apology.

My friend was not yet practiced at dealing with these types of issues, so she matched her level of offense in terms of scope by sending an email to all the people she had sent the error to, but she did not match it in terms of gravity. Her tone appeared to me, at that time, to be light and dismissive. After a few days of some back and forth, we were able to sit down and finally have an honest conversation. I explained to her how the impact of her words were damaging, although I believed in my heart that she had no malicious intent. She talked to me about her questions, worries, and concerns. We made such a connection over that talk that in the following year, she became my safe anchor in a department and school where I did not always feel accepted or appreciated. When she felt unsure about something, she no longer feared talking or asking about it. Because I saw that she cared for me and wanted to understand, I placed value on the time we spent discussing various issues. When I began teaching a new class that she had previously taught, she was the first person I talked to because I did not feel like I had to put up a mask of independence with her. I could honestly say I needed help and know that she would not judge me as incompetent as a result, because our conversations had allowed us to see each other's humanity. Funny how that works, huh?

Theologian Thomas Parker is often quoted, most famously by Dr. Martin Luther King, Jr., as saying, "The arc of the moral universe is long, but it bends toward justice." I wholeheartedly believe this. Your apology should not just be about kudos for yourself or maintaining relationships with others, but about moral justice. The actions that you took, no matter how small, may have had a ripple effect that impacted others in ways you could not foresee. Wouldn't it be nice to know that you made amends and stopped whatever long-term damage could have or would have occurred? Although people may think that is being over-dramatic, we cannot underestimate how far a simple apology can go. When we think of some of the most egregious crimes committed throughout history, many of the perpetrators can point out specific occurrences that shaped their thoughts and opinions. How many of those tragedies would have been prevented or addressed with the proper apology?

Pro Tip:
When my students were preparing for debates or group discussions, I would often have them create possible responses they could make to difficult questions or anticipated counter-arguments that the opposition might

make. Have you done the same? Have you practiced your apology?

Remember that we are actively engaged in falling in love with people of different experiences. Consider what you would do if you made your spouse or partner angry. How would you go about making amends with them? What would you do if flowers or their favorite meal didn't work? How would you show that you are truly remorseful and value your relationship with that person? Whatever your answer is, do that.

Reflection: Can you remember a time when, maybe, you did not do so well apologizing? What happened? Did you ever find out why the person was upset? How did you make amends, if you were ever able to? What would you do differently if you had a do-over?

_____

_____

_____

_____

_____

_____

_____

_____

_____

Whose Responsibility is it Anyway?

My husband and I met over twenty years ago, and when I married him, I found myself in the middle of this big, loving, and amazing family. I found myself blessed with not only my husband's immediate family, but a niece, 8 nephews, aunts, uncles, and too many cousins to count. Most of this extended family lives in Flint, MI, where my husband grew up. When, in 2015, researchers from the Environmental Protection Agency and Virginia Tech discovered that water in Flint contained dangerous levels of lead, I was angry and extremely worried.

A group of politicians and administrators in the state of Michigan had instituted cost-cutting measures that led to a political, moral, medical, and structural crisis. Because the changes did not follow water treatment guidelines, the water began to erode the pipes, which caused the iron from the water mains to leach into the water supply, turning it brown. The lead from lead pipes in many homes caused health problems ranging from effects on the kidneys, heart, and nerves to "impaired cognition, behavioral disorders, hearing problems, and delayed puberty" (CNN Library, "Flint Water Crisis Fast Facts) in children. Eventually, there was an outbreak of Legionnaire's Disease, which killed 12 people and sickened hundreds more. Several government officials were charged for their role in this travesty, and the whole time I watched for an announcement that someone was going to fix the problem. For me, this was not some remote city with unknown residents; this was my family, and I wanted to be sure they were safe.

As of early 2019, the problem has only been partially addressed through a series of programs and appropriations that temporarily help, but do not fully solve the problem of corroded pipes and untrustworthy water. When I visit certain family members, there are stacks of water bottles piled up and gallons of water for mundane tasks that we would turn on the faucet for. The people who were responsible for creating this mess are no longer in charge of it, and yet it remains a problem to be solved. Thousands of people cannot trust their water supply (which they must still pay to have) and they definitely cannot trust the people who are supposed to be protecting them from occurrences like this.

Many people wonder why this problem has not been completely fixed. It is a prime example of systemic racism at work. Flint is a city comprised primarily of African Americans. It was one of the cities that black southerners flocked to during the Great Migration in efforts to avoid lynching in the South and gain economic opportunity in the North. These individuals found high-paying jobs working in manufacturing plants such as General Motors. At its peak in 1960, Flint boasted 200,000 residents, but as of 2016, the population was less than 99,000. The majority, a full 57%, is black, including my loved ones.

When we think of the idea of responsibility for racism, I believe that this is a perfect analogy. (You can probably tell that one of my favorite teaching tools is the use of analogies, similes, and metaphors.) The people of Flint have an issue that they were not responsible for causing, but of which they suffer the consequences. The people who implemented the systems that caused the problems are no longer there to make changes. The individuals who are now in power were in no way responsible for the initial systems, but still operate that system. Citizens who should be in the streets rioting that such a tragedy has been allowed to happen in our country have personal biases that have made them apathetic to the plight of the residents of Flint. Some of these individuals may sign a petition or post their dismay on social media, but they reserve any real efforts for the causes that directly impact them.

This is exactly how systemic racism works. A system was created years ago that has not been solved, but which needs to be fixed for the sake of those impacted. No one who is affected by the system can change it without the support of those who have control over the system. No one who currently has control over the system was responsible for setting it up, but could make change if they wanted to by implementing a new system or overhauling the current one, including replacing the parts that are corroded and cause the most damage. People not impacted tend to ignore the fact that the problem has not been corrected, or assume that someone else is working on it, and therefore, place little time, energy, or passion into pressuring those with the power to make change to do so immediately.

For this reason, it becomes everyone's responsibility to make change, with the onus placed on the white community to do the heavy lifting. Racism is a problem that white people own, but from which black people suffer. The change that must take place will inevitably fall to the group that owns it.

What will this work look like? Let's think about it from the perspective of Flint. What has to be done to fix the problems in my husband's hometown?

- **Go back to receiving water from a safe source**--This was done in Oct. 2016, but the water remains unsafe. Why? Mainly because authorities did not clean out the water delivery systems. When it comes to systemic racism, this is the equivalent of implementing the Civil Rights Act of 1964 or the Supreme Court ending school segregation in the *Brown v. Board of Education* decision. It is a start to allow people access to the institutions, but there is more to do if we are going to truly fix the problem.

- **Have specialists come in and assess what procedures, rules, and processes need to be corrected**--There are people from various organizations, schools, and companies who are trained to assess water systems for weaknesses and who are more than capable of providing the people of Flint with a plan for restoring their water quality to that of neighboring towns (including the more affluent suburb of Grand Blanc). Likewise, there are trained individuals who are able to go into our systems (judicial, educational, foster care, employment, etc.) and use the data collected over hundreds of years to show us how these systems continue to uphold white supremacy and oppress people of color.

- **Place people in charge who are willing and capable of implementing these changes**--Although the people who caused this issue in Flint have been dismissed or indicted, the people who have subsequently been in charge of making changes have failed to do so. Some have been elected officials while others have been hired or appointed. No matter how they came to be in a position to effectuate change, they have all failed to do so on a large scale. The reasons why have varied from not agreeing upon next steps to being influenced by outsiders through donations or business opportunities. So, we need to be looking for people who are not only capable of creating change, but are dedicated and have been empowered to make change. We also need people who are willing to do the hard work of it. The same must happen with systemic racism.

- **Begin to deconstruct the parts of the system that have been eroded or polluted**--The water in Flint will continue to be unclean if, despite tapping into a clean water source, the services flow through contaminated pipes. Necessarily, the parts of the system that dirty the water must be removed so that Flint residents, just like Detroit residents whose water flows from the same source, can receive clean water. This remains true with our systems. Although our laws and civil rights are supposed to be equally applied, they often are not because of the pipeline through which they flow. For instance, on the surface, school funding laws seem equal, but by the time they flow down the pipelines, predominantly white schools receive thousands of dollars more per child than their predominantly black counterparts. In order to fix this systemic inequality, we must remove the portions of our laws, and the people these laws are misapplied through, that help support it.

- **Install new, clean parts and piping that will allow the clean water to flow uncontaminated through the system**--Once we install new pieces to the system, clean, uncontaminated water should begin to flow to the residents of Flint. This will be true for systemic racism, as well. Once we interrupt the racism within our systems and replace the contaminated parts with new, clean parts, we should start seeing a new flow of equality and rights to those most impacted.

- **Monitor, test, and update the new system as needed**--This will be an ongoing, regulated process. The people in charge of the system will need to keep watching and checking to make sure that it is still producing high quality water for the residents of Flint. Part of the process will include checking in with these citizens to ask them how it is working for them. Does is still taste as it should? Is it still clear? Have they noticed anything that needs changing? If anything is untoward, there should be a procedure for responding to the residents, one which includes their voices in the process. In this same way, members of minority groups must be able to use their voices to express what is working and not working for them. We must be able to say, "this change you made is producing this result." If that result is still hindering people from attaining equal rights, then changes must be made accordingly.

Just thinking about how much change our system would need seems overwhelming. When one considers all of the moving parts that must carefully and purposefully work together, it becomes even more unimaginable. However, our focus needs to be on the role that we personally can play to get other people on board while also doing all that we can. Breaking down these systems will require leaders, followers, supporters, activists, and laborers. It also requires that people remain informed and active in the cause. We need people to dismantle the pipeline, as well as people to place pressure on the people with the power to order the dismantling. When those in charge do not meet our expectations, we need individuals who are brave enough to say, "we need someone else," even if you like the person who was previously in that role. If you can find no one to be that person, we need people who are willing to learn, prepare, and then fill the void.

The book of Esther in the Bible tells of a beautiful young woman who is chosen to become one of King Xerxes' wives. When Xerxes is tricked by his counselor Haman into declaring that all the Jews in the kingdom should be killed, Mordecai (Esther's cousin who raised her after her parents' deaths) goes to her and begs her to appeal to the king for her people's lives. Esther expresses fear because appearing before the king without permission could lead to death if it displeases him.   However, Mordecai takes this time to remind her of a few important pieces of information:

1. Just because you have an elevated position, you are still subject to the fates imposed on your people.
2. If you do not stand up, someone else will, and you will still be left with the consequences of your inaction.
3. Who's to say that you have not been placed in this position for "such a time as this" (Esther 4:14)?

Even if you are not of the Christian or Jewish belief system, this story still holds a great lesson. We all have a purpose to fulfill while we are here on earth. Sometimes, the goals you accomplish and the achievements you make are not just for you alone. If you believe in the idea of the social contract, then there is a debt to be paid for those who created a place for you and put structures in place to ensure your success. Part of the debt you owe is paid through your service to others.

This partially means that what is required of you is that you contribute to bettering the system that helped you, so that others have the same opportunity to succeed that you did. Unfortunately, not all believe this to be true, so that means that you must redouble your efforts in order to even the playing field for others who, through no fault of their own, do not have the same opportunities.

Recently, I was watching an interview with California governor Gavin Newsom. In talking about taking the steps that we needed to take in order to reverse the damage we have done to our environment, he stated, "there's right and wrong, and then there's the whims of the majority." Please understand that some of the work that you will need to do will not be popular; not with your family, friends, coworkers, acquaintances, church members, etc. There will be plenty of times when you have to stand alone with only your moral compass to guide you. Yet, you must be courageous. As you can see from the Flint water crisis, the cases of police shootings, the number of people who die each year from lack of healthcare access, the number of innocent people who die in poverty or because of poverty-related conditions, it is literally a matter of life and death.

As you step into your responsibilities, I would encourage you to remember all of the following:

- Spend more time listening than speaking. My wise uncle Ray used to always tell me, "listen twice, speak once," a lesson that originated with Greek philosopher Epictetus. Even though the majority must break the systems of oppression, they cannot do so without centering the voices of the oppressed. Otherwise, we're going to keep ending up with solutions that do not address the totality of the problem. We'll remove a few pipes without finding out that there were more that needed to be replaced further down the line.

- While it is your job to listen to what impacted peoples have to say, it is not their job to do the work for you. Consider it this way. If we were problem-solving in Flint, you would need to listen to the people to find out what needs to be done, but it is not their responsibility to then tell you HOW to do it. They may tell you that the water still smells and tastes strangely, but it will fall to you to gain the education necessary to find out what might still be wrong and why. It is your job to find out what actions the previous administration took to correct the problem and where they possibly went wrong. Expecting impacted peoples to both tell you how they've been impacted and then to tell you how to deal with it is expecting them to do the labor (emotional, social, economic,etc.) for you. It is delegating your responsibility to the people who have been historically disempowered to effectuate change. You must do the heavy lifting here. There are no shortcuts that can be taken.

- Realize that while quite a bit of this work must be done individually, we also need to find allies who are willing to join with us. Together, we will be more effective. You must speak out on an individual basis, but you also need to find ways to join with others to take concerted and intentional group action. For instance, the people of Flint will need groups of people to contact their congressmen and Michigan state legislators to demand action. They will need political action committees and donations to pressure those politicians who are influenced by campaign donors in order to get commitments to effectuate change. They will need people who are willing to vote for politicians who will prioritize people over profit. All of those things will take people acting both individually and collectively.

- While you need to do your part, you must avoid developing a savior complex. Impacted communities do not need saviors; they simply need people who are willing to do their part to ensure that these communities have the opportunity to save themselves. Given the same resources, advances, and access, we are more than capable of moving forward.

- For some people, the loss of privilege will feel like oppression. You have to keep going anyway. In your mind and heart, you have to accept that you're not losing anything. When a contractor builds a stable house that a whole family will live in, they must at times take soil from one portion of the property and put it elsewhere in order to make sure that the building surface is even. Remember that during the construction process, you may lose your hill, but in the end, you'll gain something greater. The process of taking responsibility always requires individuals to remember that there is a greater good and grander reward to which you can look forward.

Pro Tip: Although I have primarily addressed race in the Flint example, this can apply to any situation of discrimination. I often tell people that we cannot trade one type of discrimination for another. I speak to race because that is what directly impacts me on a day-to-day basis, but we all have to work to disrupt any type of discrimination: Islamophobia, anti-Semitism, homophobia, misogyny, and so on.

<u>Reflection:</u> When you think about your realm of influence, where can you begin the process of taking responsibility? Basically, what's your role in fixing the system?

_____

_____

_____

_____

_____

_____ .

_____

_____

_____

Being an Ally in the Workplace

When I was growing up, my relatives' occupations covered a vast array of industries and positions. My great grandmother, the matriarch of our family, was the caretaker of the owners of the local funeral home. Though she cleaned and took care of their home, Granny also began helping to prepare the bodies for burial by doing makeup and dressing them, among other things. Through this career, she helped raise several of the members of our family in addition to her own three children. She even raised my mother, her granddaughter, for the majority of her young years. In small town Tennessee, there were only a few options available through the years, so many of my relatives ended up in factories or behind the counter at restaurants. My great uncle Ray was the first person in our family to go away to college when he went to California to attend school on a basketball scholarship. Eventually, he would inspire several people in my family to bet on education as a pathway, including me. On my dad's side, my grandfather was a respected businessman in the community, selling insurance and taking care of his wife and five children. I was able to see people in professions that ranged from farmers to factory workers, from teachers to engineers.

No matter what field of work my family members were in, I also heard the stories of racism they faced while just trying to do their jobs. At a very young age, I was introduced to the idea of the "black tax," which basically states that African Americans have to work twice as hard for half the credit. Practically every black person in America could explain that concept to you in great detail with personal examples if they were asked about it. I listened to all the stories and heard what they were saying, but did not have to think much about how I would prepare for it because I was somewhat incubated. I grew up in the same school district from second grade until I graduated high school, so the students, teachers, and administrators were well aware of my capabilities from an intellectual and leadership perspective. Throughout college and my first career in the social services, I faced other types of racism, frustrations, and setbacks, but nothing that I felt fell under the umbrella of the "black tax." It was not until I got into education that I encountered experiences which allowed me to truly understand how insidious this concept was and the impact it could have on people of color. In my predominantly white school district, I was often the only person of color in the room, and found myself challenged in ways that my colleagues were not and would not ever be because of the difference between my skin color and theirs. In many of the situations, I felt that my colleagues and administrators did not always know how to support me or the other people of color with whom they worked. I have included specific examples later on in this chapter..

When I do training in professional or public settings, a question I am frequently asked in relation to this topic is, "what do I need to do to be a good ally to people of color in my office/school/groups?" The answer is as complex and nuanced as any related to race and ethnicity. The general answer is follow the golden rule. Treat people of color how you would want to be treated. However, the issue becomes quite a bit more complex once you realize that you cannot apply that standard from a white-centered viewpoint. Most of the mistakes that well-meaning allies make are the result of not applying a cultural lens to the actions they take and the expectations they have of their colleagues of color. Practiced allies do this without thinking, but new allies have a long journey to reaching that point. Allyship is hard, characterized by mistakes, apologies, listening, and learning. If it was easy, racism would have been eradicated years ago.

For those that are in the beginning stage and feeling unsure about whether they are "doing it right," there are few things you can do and/or remember to begin your learning journey.

- **Learn and understand the difference between diversity and inclusion.** Too often, companies, organizations, and groups make the mistake of thinking that because they are diverse, they are "doing it right." However, those same groups often wonder what went wrong when they lose people of color after some time. The problem is often that while they applaud being diverse, they ignore the need to be inclusive. These are two distinctly different concepts. Diversity is the starting point; inclusion is the end goal. Diversity is a count of the people in the room; inclusion is a gauge of how those people are present in the room. Diversity applauds the differences among people, while inclusion asks whether people of diverse backgrounds are accepted and respected. Diversity considers data, while inclusion considers humanity. Diversity recruits; inclusion retains. Regardless of a person's role in their office/company/group/organization, they should be working toward inclusion.

- **Encourage your company or organization to develop a cultural inclusion goal AND a plan for implementing it.** Whether you are the person responsible for setting these goals or you are the individual who provides feedback, you should try to advocate for a stated goal. However, realize that it is not enough to just have a goal. A company that wants to be inclusive must also be intentional about the actions they will take to ensure that the goal becomes attainable. If your company does not have one and is not interested in developing one, then you must consider what steps you will take to effectuate change in your office and its culture. Never underestimate the power that you, even alone, can have.

- **Create a seat at the table if there is not one, but make sure the role is not tokenized.** Too often, people of color are not invited into the rooms where decisions are being made. The result of this can be disastrous for a company if they are not intentional. For instance, at the beginning of 2019, high fashion company Gucci came under fire for releasing a sweater that seemed to imitate blackface, and lost millions of dollars as they dealt with the backlash from this decision. In their apology, the company committed to increasing diversity throughout their organization to correct an issue prevalent in too many upper management teams. This incident served as a prime example of why representation matters and why having diversity of people, thoughts, and skills is beneficial for all businesses. If you look at your own work environment and see that not many people of color are in decision-making positions, you can be the person who suggests that your colleague of color be part of whatever committee, team, or project your employer has. However, once that person is on the team, utilize that person as you would a white colleague. Examine their strengths and then assign responsibilities that allow them to make a considerable contribution.

- **Amplify our voices.** In many organizations, people of color feel as if their voices are dismissed or not heard. A common experience I hear is that the person of color will state an idea or make an observation that is ignored until their white (often male) colleague says the same thing. A good ally not only listens when the POC speaks, but encourages others to do so, as well. It may look like asking, "Did you hear what Heather said earlier about XYZ?" Or it could look like stating openly, "Heather said the same thing earlier. We should look into what she was saying." Sometimes, it even looks like saying, "Hey, could you hold that thought? I was listening to what

Heather was saying about this issue." However it looks in a particular situation, any effort you make to acknowledge good ideas and the person uttering them will make the work environment feel inclusive of all.

- **Give credit where credit is due.** It is very important that you work to credit people of color with the work that they do, no matter how seemingly small the activity was. This becomes extremely important when managers and supervisors are able to make firing and promotion decisions. Unfortunately, these individuals are not immune to unconscious biases and can make decisions based upon perception instead of reality.

  For example, a few years ago, I began leading a social justice group at my school. The group was responsible for leading presentations that shared what we were learning about the topic with the rest of the faculty. These presentations often lasted 30 minutes or so and involved different activities that the staff could use to process ways to incorporate the knowledge into their classrooms. The social justice group often met in the library, so the librarian typically gathered the information on her computer and projected it onto the SmartBoard so we all could see it as we planned. Once the presentation was done, the librarian would send the finalized copy to the head principal so she could include it in the overall faculty meeting slide show. In March of that year, right before spring break, the principal came to my classroom to tell me that she was disappointed in my leadership. She based her opinion (partially) on her perception that I was not actively coordinating this group and involved in the planning process simply because the emails with the final presentations came from the librarian and not from me. She also based it upon the fact that an initiative she had put me in charge of was not panning out because she had not listened when I told her my department was not ready. I partially blame myself for her misconceptions because I had not actively taken credit for the work I was doing well. It allowed her unconscious biases to come through and for her assumption to be that I was not doing anything.

How might those assumptions have changed if my colleagues and allies had openly stated to her, "Heather is responsible for putting this together"? Or if they would have actively thanked me for helping their students individually or fulfilling the vision of the project at hand? The part I disliked most about all of this was that they should not have had to do any of that. The presentations we produced should have been sufficient proof of my efficacy, and credit should have been equally distributed to all of us. However, what SHOULD be true is much different from what IS true. If you want to be an ally to a person of color, be sure to be liberal in attributing credit for work well done. Do not leave it to the imagination or unconscious biases of your boss, supervisor, or manager.

- **When the person of color advocates for themselves (as they will inevitably have to do), do not dismiss what they are saying as intimidating and aggressive**. Existing as a person of color in a predominantly white atmosphere requires a lot of emotional labor. For those who have never heard that term, emotional labor is basically the additional work we have to do in order to regulate our feelings in a work environment. Alicia Grandey, an industrial-organizational psychologist, described it using this analogy.

  > "It's kind of like when you get a gift and you don't really like it, and you have to still smile and act nice because otherwise your Aunt Bernadette would be offended. But

you have to do that all day long. Not only
that, but it's explicitly part of your job. It's
tied to your wages and outcomes, and if
you don't do it, there are consequences
—like you could lose your job, or you could
get in trouble. And it's with strangers, for
the most part" (Fessler, "An Extremely
Clear Definition..."

Despite our attempts to minimize the perception
of threat and "fit in," there will inevitably be a
situation which will require us to advocate for
ourselves because the offense is so egregious that
we have reached a breaking point. When this
happens, an ally will be the person that listens and
does not dismiss what the individual is saying, and
resists attempts to paint this individual as hostile
or attitudinal.

I will never forget an incident that happened in
my first year of teaching. I came downstairs to
the common area of my school and found one of
my students crying. When I asked her what was
wrong, she said that her stomach hurt her badly,
but the school nurse wouldn't call her mother
because she didn't have a fever. I helped the
young lady up and took her back to the nurse's
office, but as soon as I walked in, the nurse's aide
spoke to me sternly, stating that they had already
seen the young lady and that they weren't sending
her home. I was furious, both because of the way
she was insensitive to the young woman's pain,
but also because of the way she had spoken to me
in front of a student. I proceeded to use a stern
tone as I told her that this young lady was
obviously in pain and that I felt her mother should
be called so that she could make the decision
about whether or not the young lady should go
home or possibly be taken to the doctor. I never
raised my voice in the process and, in fact, used
up my daily tolerance of emotional labor in order
to maintain my calm.

Despite all my effort, when the nurse's aide told the story to the other secretaries at lunch, I became a neck-rolling shrew, the stereotypical representation of the angry black woman. Thankfully, a friend who knew how I handle conflict, and had observed that I actually get quieter and less expressive when I am angry in a professional setting, was there to push back and say, "that does not sound like her at all." She was able to counteract the negative representation that this individual perceived in her interaction with me.

Though my friend was there to save the day that time, she was not there at other times, and the misperceptions of me were allowed to stand. I often wonder how many opportunities I missed out on because someone perceived that I had an attitude or was ill-tempered due to me having to stand up for myself from time to time. I'll never know, but I have been in rooms where I've been the friend who has to protect a person of color's ability to stand up for themselves.

- **Don't allow your cultural incompetency to interfere with procedure or policy (i.e. don't do something different for the person of color than you would for others because you do not feel comfortable with having a conversation with that person).** If I had a $1000 for every meeting, conversation, or memo that was created because people were too intimidated to deal with me as a person of color, I would be able to pay off my house note and student loans. The irony was that in their attempts to appear more equitable, they made it even more obvious that I was the special case they were accommodating. While it is true that equity does not necessarily mean treating someone equally, it also does not mean treating members of the minority as outside the norm.

Cultural competency will allow you to see the individual as a human being first, not a stereotype or representative. The humanity in you must recognize and celebrate the humanity in the other person, so you should consider your actions from the perspective of your own humanity. If you were already someone who may feel a bit outside of the office norms, how would you want an action handled if someone was showing you that you are valued in the work environment? Would you want an individual meeting where that person provided feedback and support, or would you want an office-wide memo to go out, even though people would know it obviously referred to you? Would you want to sit and talk to the other employee impacted, or would you want a department-wide meeting where everyone stared at you and the other employee involved because they had heard the rumors? Would you want a supervisor to not give you any feedback and allow you to do something incorrectly time and time again because they were too concerned about "saying the wrong thing" to give you tips for improvement so you could be successful? Would you want people to whisper information behind your back that they would simply address directly with others? I'm pretty sure I know the answer to all of these questions, but I want to be sure that you are considering these aspects as you think about how to be a better ally. While there will be changes and accommodations you may make for one person versus another, they should never be so drastic and obvious that you "otherize" the person you are trying to accommodate.

- **Do not expect that one person of color to be your company's diversity representative.** I cannot stress this enough! Recently, I read about the case of Sharika Robinson, a young woman who is suing the law firm she works for for misrepresenting the inclusive nature of the firm, as well as for using the minority employees as "diversity props" to impress clients and lure other minorities to positions within the company. "In reality, Robinson says, she is one of only two black associates at the 165-lawyer firm's three offices, and the firm has had no more than 10 black lawyers since 1960" (Weiss, "Firm uses minorities..."). This concern is not unique. Many minorities in predominantly white organizations find themselves in similar positions.

In both my educational and professional experience, I frequently found myself being asked to go and represent my organization, company, school, or employer in programs or meetings, only to quickly discover that my role was performative, not substantive. I was there to be the black person in the room or to have my voice used to benefit the white people, not because I was going to be utilized in any necessary function or because it benefited me.

Another problem that Ms. Robinson alleges in the lawsuit is that she "was assigned work unevenly, excluded from case discussions, assigned grunt work, and excluded from social and marketing functions, including golf and sporting events. When she complained about work assignments, the suit says, 'she was told to go to the partners and 'smile' and ask for work" (Weiss). This is also what many people of color experience, and precisely what I meant when I said earlier that the person of color's role at the table should not be tokenized. I am sure that Ms. Robinson, after having to work so hard to gain her juris doctorate degree, possessed comparable skills to her colleagues and should have been assigned an equitable amount of responsibility and perks. When a person of color is in a professional setting, they should be assigned work according to their skills and abilities, not according to a perception of them as a token. We feel the difference in treatment, responsibility, and benefits when they are not given in an equitable manner.

- **Consider certain office traditions from various lenses. What are those traditions communicating to your minority co-workers?** A few years ago, as our students began learning about and considering inclusion, student leaders took a hard look at our spirit week traditions and found that some of the themes they chose were not reaching certain students because they did not reflect the interests of all. Our school, though majority white, had members of various races, nationalities, religions, sexual orientations, etc., as essential parts of our student body. They changed several of the theme days to exclude those that were offensive and those that were culturally irrelevant for others. For example, the students made a conscious decision to do away with opposite gender day, understanding that this may be alienating our LGBTQ+ students by mocking their gender identity in the name of fun. They also changed jersey day to a sports theme day, considering that some of our students' socioeconomic statuses may not allow them to participate in a jersey day because of the cost of jerseys. Everyone could possibly participate in a sports day through a t-shirt, hat, keychain, etc. that they may already own.

These students set a great example for the type of thoughts we should be putting into our office traditions. We must consider what messages our traditions communicate to our employees and how the operate in office norms. Are bonuses, awards, promotions, or yearly reports given at the annual Christmas party, meaning that all employees, regardless of religious affiliation, must participate? Is the office decorated for St. Patrick's Day and Columbus Day, but not Cinco de Mayo or Black History Month? Do employees receive adjusted work hours or extra leave to attend Ash Wednesday services, but not to celebrate Ramadan? Do office emails acknowledge smaller observances such as Grandparents Day, but not major holidays in other religions such as Diwali and Yom Kippur? Does the company picnic feature roasted pig, hamburgers or hot dogs, but not foods that can be consumed by people with religious food restrictions? As people were planning company meetings and events, did they make sure the facility was welfare accessible and contained technology to accommodate people who are deaf/hard of hearing?

Considering your office's traditions through another lens usually requires you to think of the composition of your office and trying to think from other perspectives. It also means knowing a bit about those individuals and their individual needs as it pertains to their culture, religion, ability level, etc. For instance, do not just assume that your Muslim colleague will need time off for Ramadan. They may not practice their religion in the same way as the person you read about on the internet. Instead, go to them and say, "I know that Ramadan is coming up soon. Will you need additional time off or to adjust your schedule, like I sometimes need to for Ash Wednesday or Good Friday?" This shows both respect for their religion and their individuality. Ultimately, that is the goal you are trying to accomplish. The question you should always ask is, "what do I do to show respect for what they are (identity) and who they are (individuality)?"

- **Take time independently to learn about and understand cultural differences.** In previous chapters, I discussed the idea that people of color and members of other minority groups are not responsible for educating you. Though you can ask questions when confused, you should try to seek the information out from reliable sources as often as possible first. Also, please make sure that whatever source you select, it is one that is respected by the group being described.

Honestly, as an African American woman, I hope no one listens to the words of Candace Owens, conservative commentator and political activist, to gain insight into the thoughts, feelings, and experiences of the average African American woman. You would be misled, to say the least. Because we are not monoliths, you must also look at several sources or look at information that is a compilation of sources. This is why it is essential that we be constantly learning about one another. In her TED Talk titled "The Danger of the Single Story," Chimamanda Ngozi Adichie stresses that we must expose ourselves to several different perspectives, especially those of people whose voices are traditionally quieted or silenced.

Once you learn about another culture's traditions, it will also be necessary for you to consider how those differences in cultural norms inform perceptions of performance, efficacy, and commitment. Have you judged this person according to your own cultural standards or are you thinking about the situation from their perspective?

For example, I disliked one of my dearest friends for the first six months that I knew her. We entered employment in our school district at the same school the very same year, so we had to go through new teacher training together. One day, we ended up paired for an activity and got along really well. However, the next day when we arrived at training, she walked past me without saying anything. I felt it was a snub. I mean, I do come from the South where sharing a laugh together meant you were friends, and you speak to everyone you've previously met whether you like them or not. So I used my cultural lens to judge her as stuck up and rude. However, I would later discover that it was nothing like that. She was terrified and uncomfortable as she entered a new career in a new atmosphere far away from her hometown, so she was trying to tread lightly as she learned. Yet, because of that one event, I maintained my distance from her and viewed any attempts she made to communicate with me warily. Eventually, a mutual friend asked us both to have lunch with her (also totally unaware of my feelings), and from there we began building our friendship and clearing up the misunderstanding. Thirteen plus years later, I was blessed to officiate as she married the love of her life.

- Get into the habit of apologizing properly when you mess up. In Chapter 4, I talked about giving the proper apology. I wanted to repeat the expectation here because I cannot stress enough that as long as you are making an effort, you're going to get it wrong. When you get it wrong, apologize, accept responsibility, make amends, and make necessary changes so that you won't repeat that mistake again.

Pro Tip: Do you have a co-worker or colleague that you have already messed up with severely? Most likely, that person already views you negatively. So how do you repair your relationship? Honestly, going to that person and saying "I'm sorry, but I'm learning" will be met with suspicion, as will your going to them and trying to make small talk. The best apology is changed behavior. Start by showing this individual through your actions that you are learning. What you say won't matter as much as what you do. Want to show this individual that you support them? Instead of saying it, show it by highlighting their idea in the meeting or by asking them to be on your team AND valuing their input. It will take time, but you can do it if you remember that actions speak louder than words.

Reflection: As you consider your workplace, school, church, or organization, where is there room for improvement? What steps could you take to make it more inclusive?

_____

_____

_____

_____

_____

_____

_____

_____

_____

_____

_____

_____

_____

_____

The Subtle Racism of Lowered Expectations

People can often point out the blatant examples of racism, such as racial slurs, swastikas, or burning crosses. However, many have a much harder time identifying the subtler ways racism operates. One of these ways is the **subtle racism of lowered expectations**.

The subtle racism of lowered expectations is when your conscious/ unconscious bias causes you to expect less of a person of color because of their race. The blatant racist might automatically say "Person X obviously can't do ABC because they are (black, Indian, Japanese, etc.)," but the well-meaning, conscious "ally" can also fall into this trap. It is harder to identify because it is most often wrapped in support and care.

Some examples might be as follows:
- applauding a student of color for doing poorly or average on an assessment (at least they did it, right?) and/or not honestly assessing it for areas of improvement at the same level you would a white student. Good-hearted educators do this often for a variety of reasons (don't want students to fail, concerned about student's resilience, etc.)

- automatically explaining complex concepts to a person of color on the assumption that they don't have the requisite knowledge to engage with you. This assumption is also based on the idea that a person of color has less intelligence, education, or resources than you, so you must overcompensate for this by explaining more than you would to an "equal."

- hiring the less-qualified person over the POC because Applicant A would be "a better fit." Many times this means that you are choosing the person you will have to train and monitor more because the person of color might present challenges to the aesthetics, white-centered culture, racial sensitivity, or client base of the business or organizations. To justify the rejection of these challenges, managers and leadership name "better fit" as a choice that lowers the expectation of the amount of professionalism a person of color would bring to the table.

- questioning the credentials of POCs more than those of their white counterparts. Many people of color find themselves having to prove that they belong at the table before they can make the contributions they were trained to make.

- making comments like "you're so articulate" when a POC is highly-educated. I faced this often myself, even after I told people that my degree was in English or that I taught language arts in a prominent school district. The individuals saying this meant no harm and meant it as a compliment, but offended me nonetheless because it denied who I was as a person and replaced me with a stereotype.

- asking to speak to "someone in charge," even when the POC in front of you has indicated they have decision-making authority. When a person does this, they are asking the person of color to bring a member of the majority group to validate them. I have seen situations where the person doing the validation was the person of color's subordinate. Basically it was the equivalent of asking the part-time worker to okay the manager/owner's authority simply because the worker was white.

- dumbing down in an attempt to make a connection with a POC, such as pretending to know less than you do or using simple, slangy language. Often, these attempts use stereotypes as the foundation of the conversation.

Of course, I could give further examples, but I think the reader understands what I'm saying.

So what does one do if they fall into this trap? The most significant action is to identify how your bias impacted your interactions and responses. This is a challenging process made even more difficult by our tendency to make racism a black-and-white issue (pun intended). We see it as an evil, and therefore automatically label individuals as "good" or "bad" based upon whether they have racist or biased thoughts. In our attempts to simplify an extremely complex issue, we often shade our ability to address the shades of gray within ourselves and others.

Reminder:
Once you have considered how your bias may have impacted your responses, you should work to fix the situation at hand. This may mean reassessing that essay or making changes to support more equitable hiring practices. Most often, though, it will look like apologizing to the person you misjudged, as discussed in chapter four. I will say again: apologizing to someone you have offended is okay. In fact, it is expected. Even if it is awkward and you do not know the exact words you should say, you will make up for it with sincerity. If you are wondering if you should even mention it, the answer is yes because 99 times out of 100, the POC was immediately aware of and off put by it. If they say, "no problem" in response to your apology, please know that was said in the name of civility. It's always problematic.

However, an apology is not enough if you do not alter your thought patterns and habits after this. Mistakes should be learning experiences, and the next question you should ask after the apology is, "what should I do better next time?" The answer to this question should be the catalyst for change. If you fail to make any changes, your apology becomes a tool for repairing your conscience, but is basically worthless to the rest of us. There is no space for empty interactions when addressing such a significant issue.

<u>Reflection:</u> Can you recount a time when you, even if you meant well, may have had a lower expectation for someone because of your own expectations of their level of ability? How did it impact the ways in which you interacted with this individual? (how you assigned work, assessed performance, spoke to the individual, chose topics to discuss, etc.)

Some readers may question why I chose to address this very specific form of subtle racism. I thought it would be a gateway into understanding that racism is so insidious that we often do not think of the small ways that it impacts every aspect of our lives, regardless of race. This is one form of subtle racism, but there are more for us to consider. Our focus on blatant forms of racism limits our understanding of racism as a whole and the factors that lead to it. "Research on these factors suggests that prejudiced attitudes are not limited to a few pathological or misguided individuals; instead, prejudice is an outgrowth of normal human functioning, and all people are susceptible to one extent or another" ("The Psychology of Prejudice"). The susceptibility of all people implies that racism is not something that is only part of a "bad" person's personality and mentality. Instead, it implies that we must assess "good" and "bad" on a continuum of acceptance. The degree to which a person embraces discrimination against other groups determines where they fall in terms of their goodness. If we calibrate our moral compass so that this idea is at the center of how we judge, we will also have an easier time understanding that really good people can also have racist tendencies. The two are not diametrically opposed.

Table: *Forms of Subtle Racism* from UnderstandingPrejudice.com, sponsored by the Social Psychology Network.

Name	Primary Citations	Description of Main Features
Symbolic Racism	Kinder & Sears (1981); McConahay & Hough (1976); Sears (1988)	Symbolic racists reject old-style racism but still express prejudice indirectly (e.g., as opposition to policies that help racial minorities)
Ambivalent Racism	Katz (1981)	Ambivalent racists experience an emotional conflict between positive and negative feelings toward stigmatized racial groups
Modern Racism	McConahay (1986)	Modern racists see racism as wrong but view racial minorities as making unfair demands or receiving too many resources
Aversive Racism	Gaertner & Dovidio (1986)	Aversive racists believe in egalitarian principles such as racial equality but have a personal aversion toward racial minorities

In other chapters, I have touched on each of these types of racism. Ultimately, the understanding that I would like for each of you to have is that racism is so much more than the "n-word" or swastikas. It manifests itself in a number of ways that are not blatant and that leave too much room for people to deflect, deny, and discredit. One who hopes to be an ally is left to do two things: listen to the voices of those impacted and develop their own understanding.

Understand that denial and deflection have been consistent tools of subtle racism. Because it does not look like Ku Klux Klan rallies, lynchings, racist rants, or racial pejoratives, people are able to argue that their actions and opinions were based upon other factors, without examining how they may have been influenced by racist ideas and subtle racism. It is what allows people to wave the Confederate flag and claim that it represents cultural heritage, without examining how a major part of that culture required the subjugation and enslavement of black people. It is also what allows good people to commit racist acts with impunity and without accountability.

Emerging allies must examine both blatant and subtle forms of racism, realizing that one is much easier to identify than the other. In fact, the harder work of anti-racism is found in the gray space that is subtle racism. Because of this, you will need to research, listen, and learn to ensure that you can capture the nuances or racism and explain its extraordinary reach to others.

Talking to Uncle Bob at Thanksgiving

One of my favorite movie series is the Harry Potter series. Though some might consider them kids' movies, the entire series holds several lessons for all of us to learn when examined metaphorically. One lesson can be found in the character Voldemort and the idea of using his name. Voldemort is the representation of evil throughout the series, and countless people fight to overthrow him, with some sacrificing their lives in the process.

Voldemort partly maintains his power by making his name unspeakable with a taboo spell, meaning that if people speak his name, his followers, the Death Eaters, are able to find them and harm them. Ironically though, he is defeated partially due to the fact that Harry, the protagonist of the series, is unafraid to speak his name, which leads to his capture and a series of events that ensure Voldemort's defeat.

Racism and discrimination also maintain their power through being unspeakable. People are taught that it is one of those topics to avoid at all costs, much like politics, sex, and religion. However, in the avoidance, we consistently miss the opportunity to dispel fear and put into motion the events that will lead to racism's defeat.

In her book *Why I'm No Longer Talking to White People About Race*, Reni Eddo-Lodge states, "Every voice raised against racism chips away at its power. We can't afford to stay silent." At this point, I hope that I have made clear that discussing race is not optional. We cannot vanquish racism as long as it remains unnameable, taboo, and frightening. We have to reduce its power to scare and control us on a personal level.

What you will find is that approaching conversations about race is similar to approaching a hippogriff. Much like the half-eagle, half-horse creatures in Greek mythology and *Harry Potter and the Prisoner of Azkaban*, if you do not show discussions of race the proper respect, you may meet with its sharp beak and talons. That does not mean that you simply avoid discussions of race, but instead learn, as Harry and Hermione did, how to properly honor it, and therefore, be able to engage with it as often as needed.

Throughout my years of educating people on how to talk about race, I have discovered that in order for the discussions to be the most productive, six agreements must be at play, whether spoken or unspoken:

1. Trust and speak personal experience.
2. Question broad narratives based in stereotypes.
3. Listen to understand, not to respond.
4. Reject shame, but process guilt.
5. Be comfortable with being uncomfortable.
6. Be further along in the journey than when you began.

When I lead formal discussions of race or engage with small groups, I am always sure to introduce these agreements and ask participants if they are willing to agree to them. To make sure there is no misunderstanding about what they are agreeing to, I am sure to explain each, as follows:

Trust and speak personal experience.
When we enter these types of conversations, we must speak from our personal experience. We cannot understand how racism and discrimination operates within our own lives if we are trying to speak to other people's experiences and examples. The best way to avoid this is to use "I" statements as often as possible. Instead of "people think...," directly state what you think. Also, speak about specific situations you had with specific people. In this way, you avoid broad general statements, many of which will likely imply bias.

It will also be important that you listen to and trust other people's experiences, especially those of members of marginalized groups. I have been in way too many conversations where I have shared my stories of facing racism and discrimination, only to have the person try to deny or discredit what I am saying. They did this not because I was not credible, but because they were uncomfortable or wanted to deny racism by denying my story. I often have to remind people that my experience and their experience can exist in the same space. Just because you do not experience something does not mean that it does not exist. Taking time to listen and process what I have told you about my experience takes nothing away from your own.

Question broad narrative based in stereotypes.
We always need to question broad narratives when it comes to any group and compare that against what the research, data, and statistics say. For instance, when anyone is discussing issues in the black community, inevitably someone will mention absent black fathers and attempt to progress this as the reason for any variety of problems. However, that narrative is a myth, based upon stereotype. In fact, the Centers for Disease Control's of Vital Statistics did a study in 2013 to examine

how involved fathers were in the lives of their children with whom they did not live. The study found that black fathers were even more active than white fathers in this circumstance, which goes against that broad narrative.

If you encounter one of these narratives in your discussions of race, you need to address it. Allowing the stereotype to remain unchecked or unexamined means that you will be discussing a nonexistent issue and misinterpreting the actual issues. More than that, you will be reinforcing and confirming the racism that you are trying to dismantle. Focus the individual on facts by asking them if they have a resource you can access or by looking the information up for yourself.

Listen to understand, not respond.
My wise uncle Big Ray used to always remind me to "listen twice, speak once," a colloquialism based upon the words of Greek philosopher Epictetus. We should be trying to listen to gain knowledge and understanding. While not every person has something to teach, you have to listen to know if they do or not. When I was in the classroom, I would teach my children about the three elements of Plato's rhetorical triangle: ethos (appeal using writer's authority and credibility), pathos (emotional appeal to audience's values and interests), and logos (appeal to your audience's intelligence). One idea I would stress to them is that you will not know which appeal will be most effective or what types of information will have the most impact unless you know your audience. You cannot know who you are speaking to unless you listen first.

Listen to people's complete statement. Wait a second. Think about what they said and the best way to address it. If there is no need for a response, then do not say a word. If you do respond, do not negate other people's experience, even if you've never been in that situation. If it is something that you do not understand or that you have not experienced, then ask additional questions to make sure you are clear. When you are ready to move forward, you can do so with actions that support the fact that you want to learn more about an experience you have not had, and with which you are unfamiliar.

Pro Tip: In the above, I am basing my advice on the assumption that you are engaged in a cross-racial conversation with a person from a marginalized group, and that this individual is speaking from a point of knowledge about issues and concerns related to their group. If you are conversing with a fellow white person, you must assess which techniques are best. If this person is also trying to practice anti-racism, it will look much different than a conversation with a white person who has unexamined conscious and unconscious biases, or a member of a marginalized group who has internalized their oppression.

Reject shame, but process guilt.
In the second chapter, I spoke to you about shame and guilt. Remember that shame breeds guilt and is an emotion that we really can't use because of how we react to shame and the feeling of threat:

- <u>Move away</u>--withdraw, hide, silence ourselves, keep secrets

- <u>Move toward</u>--seek to appease and please

- <u>Move against</u>--try to gain power over others, by being aggressive, and by using shame to fight shame.

None of these reactions end up being helpful if your shame prevents you from practicing vulnerability, which leads to connection with others.

Guilt is more useful because it allows you to focus on the behavior and realize that you can correct past behavior and change for the future. Processing your guilt over past actions allows you to move out of defense mode and into planning mode. What can be done to make sure this does not occur in the future? What has this incident, combined with my new knowledge, taught me? These behaviors and questions lead to the type of dialogue within which we need to engage.

Be comfortable with being uncomfortable.

Everytime I think about this concept, I think about the scene in *Indiana Jones and the Temple of Doom* where Short Round looks at Willie and says, "Hang on, lady! We going for a ride!" This is definitely a ride! It is like traveling 22 hours by car to Miami with four kids: your three children, plus your bonus child. I give that specific example because my husband and I have done that, and it was...uncomfortable, to say the least. However, once we arrived, we had the time of our lives, and that trip continues to be a memory we will cherish.

You must remember that this is not about comfort. Ensuring that white people experience comfort is part of what keeps us stuck in a never-ending cycle of inaction, so you must be willing to sit in that discomfort and experience it. Ask yourself why you feel uncomfortable at that moment. Is it because you are in unfamiliar territory? Is it because you feel personally attacked? Is it because shame and guilt is creeping in? You should never approach this with the idea that you will be comfortable. Feeling uncomfortable is assurance that you are properly engaging in the growth process.

I often think of it like this. Two of my nephews (Ricky and Jimmel, named after their dad and my husband) are body builders. They do awesome work to not only train themselves for competition, but to also help train others. Even they, when pushing to the next level, will complain that they are sore and that something was difficult. However, they accept that they must be comfortable with that discomfort if they are GOING to reach the next level. It's not enough to simply want; you have to deal with the side effects that will come as you learn.

I want to make a distinction, though, between discomfort and safety. While an individual must experience some discomfort when engaging in challenging conversation or deep reflection, honesty will be impossible if they feel unsafe. This is an inescapable aspect of human nature that we must consider as we are building allies. To build safety, you must be transparent about your intentions for the conversation, be willing to be vulnerable throughout the discussion process, and use your emotional IQ to gauge when the person may need to return to connective questions or receive warm feedback. Though we wish we could go full throttle, white fragility and human nature does not always allow us to do so. Instead, we must balance the need for the other person's safety with our sense of urgency and find the sweet spot that will gain an accomplice in our work of dismantling oppressive systems.

Be further along in your journey than you were when you began.

Dr. Maya Angelou (whom I call Mother Maya) once said, "I did then what I knew how to do. When I knew better, I did better." This process is about growth and learning how to better support marginalized groups and break down the systems that brought us to these circumstances. Each conversation you have should bring you closer and closer to your full realization as an ally and provide you with the knowledge necessary to create more allies. So, learn, grow, and do better.

Each of these tips have more to do with what should be happening internally if you are going to properly engage externally. They also are about helping you to understand what the other person might be feeling when they respond one way or the other. As you become more practiced, you will be able to sense when people are rejecting one or more of these agreements and make adjustments accordingly.

Until then, many people may need specific information about what to do as you begin having these conversations with others. When I train, I always start by providing people with information about what they should be doing before I give them tips about what they should be saying.

Doing
- Listening, listening, listening!
- Questioning.
- Reminding yourself that this is not about shaming and blaming. We have to understand what's really going on or "what it is." When you begin to feel shame responses arising, remind yourself of this mantra: NO SHAME, NO BLAME; IT IS WHAT IT IS. We have to focus on discussions of what is occurring to keep groups marginalized.

Saying
- Questioning. In my years of study and research, I have come across three questions that confront without being confrontational:
  - What do you mean? (asks person to clarify their claims)
  - How do you know? (asks person to identify their sources)

- What more should I know?/How did you conclude that? (asks person to clarify their thought process)
- Oops and Ouch method
  - Oops--I've made a mistake and would like to start over (should be accompanied by an apology).
  - Ouch--You've said something that caused me concern (should be accompanied by a short explanation).

Another important aspect to remember is that many people will be novices at discussing race. If they are at least willing to engage in the process, we should value their good intentions, provide constructive feedback, and give warm support as needed to reinforce their safety while not feeding their comfort. We also need to remember that impact trumps intent. Even if we are trying to provide them with safety, we should not, and cannot, let them escape accountability for their harmful words and actions, despite their intentions.

But what about Uncle Bob at Thanksgiving?

The holidays are approaching, and you are really looking forward to seeing your family members and catching up. Your favorite cousin will be there, as well as your aunt/uncle who will do or say something that will keep you and your husband/children/siblings laughing for years. You'll get a taste of your favorite pie, and enjoy all of the laughter and happiness that family can bring.

The only problem will be Uncle Bob...dear Uncle Bob who watches alternatively-factual news shows and listens to and accepts ahistorical information as support for his racist/discriminatory/hateful viewpoints. You look so forward to spending this time with your loved ones, but you know that you'll have to hear comments that go against everything you are learning as an ally and advocate. More than that, if you say anything, you risk the chance of angering your other family members.

What do you do?

This is yet another question that I am often asked when I do training programs. The answer is usually not what the questioner hoped because it is based on so many contingencies. The tips I have given you above will work with some people, but probably not with Uncle Bob. He is perfectly happy with his viewpoints and really does not want to hear other alternatives. This ends up being your greatest frustration because it is so obvious that he knows next to nothing about the groups against which he's discriminating.

I have found that developing an understanding of the people who tend to have this type of mentality serves two purposes for you: first, it helps you to better understand your audience so that you can be more persuasive, and secondly, it helps you to calm your anger and frustration so that you can use that energy intentionally towards more positive results and when it is most effective.

Before you begin your discussion, you must assess the audience before you. How open will the individual be to this type of conversation? While it is important that you talk to even the most resistant person, the reality is that some people are not open to it, no matter how nicely you say it or how knowledgeable you are about the subject. Some people have been so convinced that their standpoint is correct that they will not accept any outside influence or alternative viewpoints.

Remember when I mentioned earlier that some of this resistance comes from a natural human instinct? In

Blindspot: The Hidden Biases of Good People, psychologists Mahzarin Banaji and Anthony Greenwald credit this tendency to mindbugs-- "ingrained habits of thought that lead to errors in how we perceive, remember, reason, and make decisions" (Banaji and Greenwald 4). Basically, when our minds do not have enough information to form a complete picture, we fill it in using previous thought patterns and information. Considering the fact that so many white people live self-segregated experiences that have not allowed them to gather factual information about marginalized people, most of that "filler" comes from biased sources or stereotypical representations of these people.

Like Uncle Bob.

This is why you must assess time vs. value. If you argue with him for two hours, will he change his mind? How about three hours? Whatever your decision, I want you to be clear about this: it is still your responsibility to say something. This is not a get-out-of-jail-free card! The answer to this question just informs HOW you will engage. Once you make the decision to become an ally, you must always address discrimination and misrepresentations of minority groups. It will be hard, especially if you come from a family who does not discuss these types of things openly, but as I've said before, if this was easy, we would have already solved these problems.

If you decide not to have this conversation, you should still firmly and clearly state that you disagree with that person's standpoint, do not want to expose your children to pejorative language, and will not listen to that type of misinformation. Even if you are choosing not to address it fully at that moment, you should still try to make it uncomfortable for that person to say anything untoward in your presence. I understand that this will possibly lead

to furious text messages from your mother or a stern
warning from your father, but you must consider that this
is not about comfort; it is about morality. I personally do
not have the luxury of ignoring racism, because it doesn't
ignore me. I need my friends and allies to be willing to
step up and speak out for me and my children every time,
not just when they feel like it.

Sometimes, you will find yourself in a position where you
have chosen not to engage with the person, but the fact
that you have clearly stated your opposition to their
words will cause them to try to engage. In those
situations, I resort to one of two questions for them:

- Are you here to argue or understand?
- Do you want to win or learn?

The next line in the sand that I usually draw for them is
letting them know that I will willingly engage in
conversation if they wish to listen and learn, but that I
will not go back and forth justifying my (or my friends')
experiences.

The takeaway for you in this situation should be this:
Uncle Bob will probably not change until he is forced to
do so. You want to know what causes the most change?
Relationships. It can change the most hardened racist
into an ally. The story of Derek Black is proof of the
power of a relationship to transform a person. Black is
the son of Don Black, a white nationalist who founded
Stormfront.org (a propaganda website to further white
nationalist ideology). Following in line with his father and
his godfather, David Duke, Black was a rising star in the
white nationalist party and had a popular podcast series
that pulled plenty of supporters. Eventually though, he
decided to go to a liberal arts college and was able to hide
his identity as a white nationalist for a couple of years
until one of his fellow classmates outed him on a college
message board. At the time, he was away in Germany for

a study abroad semester, but when he returned home, many of his classmates wanted to ostracize him from all aspects of college life. However, Matthew Stevenson, the only Orthodox Jew at the school, decided to invite Black to his weekly Friday night shabbat dinners. Surprisingly, Black accepted his offer and showed up with a bottle of red wine.

When he arrived, Black somewhat expected to face a hostile group. Instead, he found himself integrated into the regular conversation. He sat and listened, joined in occasionally, and left at the end of the night having enjoyed himself, so much so that he came back the next week...and the week after that...and so on.

It took quite a while (I believe almost three years), but eventually he realized that, thanks to his friends, his understanding of the diverse people he was taught to hate was different than what he had learned about them. No online argument, push back at family dinner, or angry email would have changed his views at all, no matter how well-reasoned or prepared those arguments were.

So how do you bring Uncle Bob around? You may be able to by introducing him to the beauty of diversity. You may be able to bring him around diverse people (as long as he does no harm) and let him meet some new friends. However, you may just have to accept that Uncle Bob is too set in his ways, so you need to focus your energy on those individuals who do have the potential for change. This is a numbers game. The person who brings the most allies wins.

Reflection: Who is your "Uncle Bob"? What types of things have they said in the past which angered you?

How did you handle it at that time, and what do you wish you would have done differently?

_____

_____

_____

_____

_____

_____

_____

_____

_____

_____

_____

_____

_____

_____

Understanding Black Anger

Several years ago, I began teaching African-American History and Literature in a predominantly white suburban school. Truthfully, I had no experience or qualifications whatsoever to be teaching this specific class beyond being African American and an English Language Arts teacher. My concentration for my language arts degree had been British Literature, so I was better prepared to teach *Beowulf* than Baldwin or the Burundi people. I had to do quite a bit of research in order to tackle this new territory.

During this time, I stumbled upon a quote that caused me to pause and do a considerable amount of reflection. James Baldwin, in one of his many writings, stated, "To be a Negro in this country and to be relatively conscious is to be in a rage almost all the time." I sat with those words for a long time and reflected upon my entire experience as an African-American woman through this particular lens, which was telling me that *our rage was justified*.

The idea of justified rage was a new concept to me. For most of my life, race relations had been spoken of in terms of forgiveness, pacifism, celebration of advances, and "feel good" moments. Yes, African Americans often discussed their anger at various circumstances behind closed doors, but the general American population frowned upon displays of black anger in public arenas. Whenever public rage was discussed, people invoked Dr. Martin Luther King, Jr.'s philosophy of pacifism and uttered phrases like, "Dr. King wouldn't want this." For this reason, black rage, when it has erupted in the forms of riots, violence, and even community activism, has been swiftly and firmly dealt with by our systems.

In her book *Eloquent Rage: A Black Feminist Discovers Her Superpower*, Rutgers professor Brittany Cooper discusses how white society sees and reacts to these protests, stating, "Black anger, black rage, black distress over injustice is seen as, one, unreasonable and outsized; and, two, as a thing that must be neutralized and contained quickly" (Bates, "When Civility is Used...") In addition to trying to contain protests, the effort is made to reduce the emotions that we feel because of injustice, changing the conversation to make it about civility, community, or patriotism instead of addressing the injustice that caused the anger.

Take for example the Colin Kaepernick kneeling "controversy." During the events of Ferguson, one consistent phrase black people heard was that of "peaceful protest." People saw the violence and destruction that erupted after the death of Mike Brown and almost immediately began attempting to quell black anger without addressing the social conditions that sparked the anger. The idea of peaceful protest was used to reject, control, rebuke, and castigate as we entered a period of protests across the nation in response to the death of black people at the hands of police officers.

Kaepernick found a way to peacefully protest these deaths by kneeling during the playing of the National Anthem. Mind you, his protest was partially informed by a Green Beret named Nate Boyer, who noticed that Kaepernick was originally remaining seated in protest. He asked him to kneel because, "Soldiers take a knee in front of a fallen brother's grave, you know, to show respect. When we're on a patrol, you know, and we go into a security halt, we take a knee, and we pull security." Despite all of this, the backlash from white NFL fans resulted in Kaepernick losing his quarterback position and being blackballed. Most expressed that their anger was because they felt he was disrespecting veterans and their sacrifices by kneeling.

The stated message was "you can protest, but not that way." However, considering that no form of protest from walking across a bridge in Selma, AL, to sitting at lunch counters, to marching to the doors of the courthouse in Clayton, MO, to kneeling during the National Anthem has been acceptable, the implied message is, "just don't protest." Whether you agreed with the protests or not, you have to agree that the conversation ended up being shifted away from the stated purpose of Kaepernick's protest to a conversation that dismissed black anger in order to focus on white anger.

This is not healthy. This is a remnant of a destructive system that required enslaved African American men and women to accept their circumstances no matter how violent, unfair, and damaging. This is an attempt to continue to control a population by controlling its ability to respond to their condition. This is another way for the majority to claim plausible deniability when anger is expressed in more unhealthy ways. Most significantly, this causes millions of people to turn that anger inward rather than expressing it outwardly toward those responsible.

When I provide training and development to people and organizations, I often share my personal stories of racism, microaggressions, and other slights. I share from the perspective of someone who has been provided access to and earned a variety of opportunities and who has met with success and achievements that should have, according to our country's narrative, incubated me from racial discrimination. My path has followed the "all you have to do" narrative closely: I graduated high school as a top scholar and leader; I attended a competitive college on a full academic scholarship; I received my bachelor's degree, teacher's certification, and master's degrees; I married a wonderful man and am currently raising three great kids with him as my partner and friend; I have wildly supportive parents, siblings, family, and friends; and I entered "respectable" fields professionally (public service and education). Yet, I still regularly experience the same racism and fear that my skin folk of lesser means and opportunities experience. I share my experience as someone who is still funny, pleasant, optimistic, and loving, but who also understands the rage that some people have bubbling steadily, waiting for the moment they will allow it to spill over.

Once I came across Baldwin's quote, I allowed myself to also share my experiences from the perspective of someone who lives with anger that sometimes rises to the surface in unexpected ways. I remember one night, I was chatting on the phone with my sister while walking to my car from shopping at Dollar General. A woman and her daughter were walking next to me, and the woman felt it was okay to chastise me about something. I can't even remember what it was, but at that moment, my rage erupted in such a way that even my sister was shocked and surprised. The reality was that I was, too. I left the situation slightly embarrassed, but also relieved. It was like catharsis for me. After all these years of being polite and conciliatory, my anger felt good and brought a release that allowed me to again be polite and conciliatory in my next situation.

In an essay titled "Aggressive Encounters & White Fragility: Deconstructing the Trope of the Angry Black Woman," which she co-authored with Trina Jones, Professor Kimberly Jade Norwood included a Facebook post she made after an encounter she had in a local Home Depot. She describes how a white man entered her personal space to yell at her that he was next in line (he wasn't) and ends her story by stating, "So--yes, an angry black woman was in Home Depot on Manchester in West County today. BUT she had a RIGHT to be angry...and please, don't write a comment telling me that I spent more time on this post than it is worth. I get to decide what parts of my life I want to share" (Jones and Norwood). When I read her words, I felt that (as the kids say). You see, I know this woman. I educated her children and sat across from her at too many Parent Teacher Conferences to count. She is kind. She is brilliant. She is amazing. Above all, she is entitled to agency over her emotions. Despite attempts by the majority to quell black anger, there comes a point when allies must stand up and speak to the idea that our anger is justified.

In Dr. Norwood's example, what struck me most is that her anger came as a result of the anger another white male customer displayed toward her. She did nothing in the situation to warrant his anger other than speaking up for herself. She had already remained quiet and calm after one microaggression had occurred and was simply waiting to receive services from a Home Depot associate when this situation happened. This man perceived he had a right to something that he did not and proceeded to be disrespectful toward her in the process. Despite this, she knew that the people in Home Depot that night would only see her reaction as an angry black woman, not his anger which triggered hers.

Too often, this is the position that black women especially find ourselves in. We have to gauge how our anger, justified or not, will be perceived by those around us, particularly in professional situations. I mention black women especially because we face a different predicament in society than other groups. "...[C]onflating the experiences of Black women with those of Black men or white women--or assuming that Black women's concerns will be addressed in one-dimensional discussions of race or gender--renders the harms that Black women face invisible" (Jones and Norwood). Even in how we experience, process, and express anger, we see a separation from that of white women and black men, both of whom maintain a privilege (white or male) not afforded to black women. Professor Kimberle` Crenshaw introduced this idea as *intersectionality*. For black women, discrimination is experienced because of judgments of both their race and their sex. This means that we must examine impacts for black women as separate and unique.

In asking you to consider intersectionality, I am not at all asking you to dismiss the experiences of discrimination felt by white women or black men. I am asking you to understand that we need to examine these issues from three separate perspectives. You will then realize how many of our movements have tendency toward ignoring black women, though many of them have been started, supported, or propelled by that very group. We have seen this happen for more than a hundred years, through the suffragist movement, the Civil Rights movement, the #MeToo movement, white feminism and the Women's March, and the focus of black male lives in the Black Lives Matter movement (despite it being started by black women and black queer women). All were/are worthy causes that often forget that black women have specific issues that need to be seen and addressed, as well.

The idea of intersectionality becomes significant when you are processing black anger, because one begins to realize that important differences may exist in cause, triggers, reaction, processing, and expression. The reasons a black man may have for becoming angry may in part be informed by his identity as a man as well as his identity as a black person. The solutions and policies that might benefit white women may maintain the status quo for black women or produce a negative impact. How a black woman expresses anger may have a different impact on her professional and social prospects than a black man because of the intersectionality of her sex. We cannot apply just one lens when the situation involves black women, but must look through both a feminist and anti-racist lens at the same time to create policy and procedures that do not erase black women.

I have chosen, because of my work in equity and inclusion, to remain polite and conciliatory in my behavior. However, I believe that part of my work is making sure that people understand fully why some others are angry and distrustful, and why they have every right to be. Understanding black anger is a necessary part of the equity process. If one is to ever consider themselves aware of the social condition of minority populations, they must engage in understanding the emotional and behavioral outcomes of that condition. The best way to ask them to do so is to personalize it to their own experience. I often ask them to use their imagination as I present a few scenarios to consider:

- Imagine if your daily experience was filled with personal slights and passive-aggressive behaviors in almost every environment except your home.

- Imagine if you had to continuously assess your environment for safety (emotional, physical, professional, academic, etc.).

- Imagine if you were consistently treated as less than regardless of your accomplishments, education, and humanity.

- Imagine if you had to assume responsibility for not just yourself, but for every crime, mistake, or negative action committed by members of your entire race.

- Imagine having to accept all of the pain and dysfunction of almost every person who looks like you.

- Imagine a consistent feeling of helplessness and loss of hope.

- Imagine even simple things like going to the grocery store or performing your duties at work being marred by people exercising their perceived privilege over you and your body.

- Imagine if every attempt to address these circumstances was met with dismissiveness or antagonism.

- Imagine if all of these things were part of your daily experience.

It's often not just one thing that leads to this type of anger, but all of it combined.

Reflection: At what point would you feel angry and need to express anger? Which of these situations might be your "breaking point"?

_____

_____

_____

_____

_____

_____

_____

_____

_____

My hope is always going to be that we communicate in an efficient and effective manner. However, this is not possible if one does not understand and accept that black anger will likely be part of this conversation, as it should be. If we are to practice the empathy and vulnerability necessary to create change, we must be willing to share in the full range of emotions that will come with delving below the surface. Anyone who hopes to be considered an ally must learn how to function within the discomfort of that anger without issuing cries of "not me" or "not all white people." They will learn to wade through the anger until they get to the source of it. It is a difficult process, and it is only for those who are strong enough to practice vulnerability and radical love. They will do so with the realization that people of color have had to navigate white anger their entire lives as a matter of survival and safety.

Please note that my acceptance of the ability to access the full range of my emotions comes with a known price. I am at times viewed as irrational, over-emotional, "ghetto," attitudinal, unprofessional, or "uppity." My anger makes it easier for some to dismiss me because they judge me by society's stereotype rather than their own empathy and my humanity. I know that when I leave, adjectives will be assigned to me that I may or may not deserve. However, I am always proud to be able to say, "I did not allow this disrespect or discrimination to stand in my presence." Yet, I know that the price might be loss of opportunities, misperceptions of my personality, poor judgements of my talents and abilities, and, possibly, my safety. So, even as James Baldwin freed me to be angry, I must maintain my sense of self-protection. Anger, no matter how righteous, is often viewed as a threat and has cost too many of my fellow African Americans their lives.

Pro Tip: Black anger will appear in conversations about racism, will be directed at a particular person who has displayed problematic behaviors, or will be centered on the systems and public figures that perpetuate racism and inequality. Black anger may also present itself as a general distrust of people of other races. It is justified anger marked by truth-telling and displayed in the hopes that people will be enlightened and will understand the reasons behind the anger. A good ally will learn to identify righteous anger and respond to it with radical love.

What does radical love look like in the face of black anger? Give examples of words, phrases, and actions a person could use in order to be an ally and a friend.

_____

_____

_____

_____

_____

_____

_____

_____

BEING ANTI-RACIST

Why do racism and discrimination continue to have such a stranglehold on the United States? Why haven't the advancements of people of color been enough to dispel stereotypes? The answer to this question is so complex that we could spend countless years discussing it while failing to make further progress. However, it is critical that we keep moving forward with an urgency that doesn't allow us to dwell in the mundane aspects of discrimination.

In Ibram X. Kendi's book *Stamped from the Beginning*, he discusses the idea that "The history of racial ideas...is the history of ...three distinct voices--segregationists, assimilationists, and anti-racists--and how they each have rationalized racial disparities, arguing why whites have remained on the living and winning end, while blacks remained of the losing and dying end" (Kendi 2). The first two schools of thought have been used by whites regardless of their perspectives on the issue of race or their intentions, good or bad. It is time for us to let those ideals go and strive instead to be anti-racist.

Simplistically, anti-racism is being against racism. Many people can claim that they are against racism, but to actually be anti-racist requires much more than this. Many assimilationists are also against racism, but their unconscious biases remain unexamined as they attempt to address racism. They continue to operate from a place that centers white cultural norms and tries to incorporate minorities into society while maintaining white privilege. Anti-racism requires a much more complex examination of our society, systems, and constructs. It actively works to identify racism in every portion of our society, learn how it operates to support our systems, and intentionally dismantle it so that we can build an equitable society. It demands more than tolerance; it demands inclusion and the removal of privilege, not as punishment but as fair. Anti-racism is the moral result of loving all those around them and wanting them to have access to every part of society at a level equal to the white majority.

Becoming anti-racist is a growth process that is not for the weak or the fearful. You may find yourself distanced political, socially, and morally from friends and family members that you were previously close to, as long as you remained silent. Despite this, you must remember that for minority groups, silence is not an option. Our very lives depend on people not remaining silent anymore.

Anti-racism is much more than being non-racist. Someone who is non-racist pats themselves on the back for not using a pejorative, but doesn't challenge others when they do. Non-racists champion specific causes that support people of color, but never examines how their own daily interactions may be filled with microaggressions toward those same people. Non-racism is very passive in nature, while anti-racism is active and intentional. Non-racism supports systemic and individual racism through non-action, while anti-racism proactively seeks to dismantle each.

In considering non-racism as a concept, I am reminded of the words of Bishop Desmond Tutu, "If you are neutral in situations of injustice, you have chosen the side of the oppressor." Non-racism means that you see that there is injustice present in our society, in our schools, in our institutions, and in our neighborhoods, but you choose to do nothing about it. Your feeling that it is wrong does little to help, because the oppressor is allowed to continue without any opposition from those who may have the power, voice, and resources to effectuate change.

To be anti-racist, you must be introspective and come to some realizations and understandings, but more than that, you must take action based upon your realizations. Below, I have listed just a few ideas and action steps that I would like for you all to consider as you dive deeper into what it means to be an ally/accomplice in this fight against injustice.

Understand the foundations upon which racism is built. Ibram X. Kendi states that "Hate and ignorance have not driven the history of racist ideas in America. Racist policies have driven the history of racist ideas in America" (Kendi 9). Many times, these racist policies were created to indulge someone's greed and the racist ideas trickled down to common men who had no part in creating these policies. Let's take our schools, for example . The policies that have created unequal access to resources and funding for schools districts, when combined with housing policies that create concentrated areas of poverty, have led to de facto segregation within our educational systems. Because schools with fewer resources and less funding tend to be predominantly black, the racist idea that has emerged is that black students are not as intelligent and do not care as much about academic success. In this way, racist policy has fueled racist ideas about black students.

When viewed this way, it is easier for people to understand what racism truly is. Too often, white people tend to spend too much time proclaiming that they are not racist. Trainers and educators attempting to address racism and the privileging of whites must prepare for "common white responses [including] anger, withdrawal, emotional incapacitation, guilt, argumentation, and cognitive dissonance (all of which reinforce the pressure on facilitators to avoid directly addressing racism) (DiAngelo 55). The problem with this is that we will not move forward until we do directly address racism.

I hope that over the course of this book, you've learned to trust me quite a bit. It will mean that what I'm about to say next will be accepted thoughtfully as a truth rather than an aggression. Ready?

The technical definition of racism is prejudice plus power. This means that individuals took their prejudice against a racial group and used their power to discriminate against that group, such as the creating racist policy and practice within the institutions over which they had control. As a result of those racist policies, racist ideologies began to form, and those ideologies played out in the form of individual racism, which in turn upholds and reinforces systemic racism.

So when we talk about the idea of racism as it presents itself in our society, we have to realize that we are living in the midst of a continual racism factory. We are canaries in a racist mine, breathing in daily the racist ideas created by 400 years of racist policy. Are all of us touched in some way by racism? Yes. Can all of us be racist as a result? No. People of color have been prevented (through racist policy) from having any control over the systems that create racist ideas. If a person of color is angry at white people as a whole, it is more than likely not because of a racist idea created by a racist system that has now led to individual racism. It is most likely the result of lived experience that has made that person hostile toward the group of individuals who look like the people oppressing them.

In understanding what racism is, we are also able to understand that the blatant acts of racism we see, such as the events of Charlottesville, and white people calling the police on black people for doing mundane actions, are just symptoms to a much larger system of racism. The far-right wingers like those in Charlottesville are dismissed as evil and obviously racist, but I am certain that some of the people who called the cops on innocent black people would not have labeled themselves racists or placed themselves in the same category. However, regardless of severity and intent, each took racist actions as the result of the same ideas generated through racist policy.

Racism is insidious. It touches all parts of our lives, rather we would like it to or not. No matter how we label it, how often we talk about it, or if we acknowledge it, it is there because of how our society socializes and normalizes it in many ways. We cannot begin to break it down if we only examine the symptoms and not the causes. We cannot obliterate it if we keep arguing about the semantics of it instead of the substance. For this reason, we need to change the discussion in such a way that people are concerned about BEING racist much more than they are about BEING LABELED racist. When you truly understand how pervasive racism is, you will understand that being called racist is the least of our problems.

Understanding what it means to be a person of color in this society means understanding what it means to be white. Whiteness is relational to blackness or Native American-ness or any other racial minority status. To attempt to understand one without examining the other is like attempting marriage counseling, but only discussing one spouse's concerns and issues. In general, whiteness is "the processes and practices [that] include basic rights, values, beliefs, perspectives , and experiences purported to be commonly shared by all but which are actually only consistently afforded to white people" (DiAngelo 56). Whiteness is the way in which structural advantages show up in our everyday life and experiences. By not examining whiteness, people ignore the ways that blackness and other minority experiences are caused by systemic racism and majority privilege. We use coded language that focuses on the minority impact instead of the majority cause.

The tendency to not examine whiteness also allows for the continued insulation of white people from racial stress. When cause, blame, examination, and responsibility for correction can be moved to an outside source, individuals can continue to live as they always have, not making any concrete change in the process. "Because whites live primarily segregated lives in a white-dominated society, they receive little or no authentic information about racism and are thus unprepared to think about it critically or with complexity" (DiAngelo 58). Failure to examine whiteness in a segregated society leads to consistent and damaging misunderstandings of what it means to be a minority. The anti-racist is one who knows that reflectively examining their own experience is just as important as listening to others.

Being anti-racist does not mean being anti-white. We live in an either/or society. If you support something, it must mean that you are automatically against something. If the issue is related to race, people have a tendency to attempt to appeal to white fears by making the "against" something that white people often greatly support. One significant example of this is the Black Lives Matter movement. Though it was created after the death of Trayvon Martin, it really came to the forefront after the death of Michael Brown in 2014. Although it openly stated it purposes and platforms, the Black Lives Matter organization and movement somehow became a symbol of anti-police sentiment. People who wanted to show their support of police officers began flying "Blue Lives Matter" flags and placed police officers as the antithesis of black citizenry.

For me as an African American woman, it was an insult to my intelligence and a distortion of my viewpoints. I wholeheartedly support Black Lives Matter. Their sole purpose is to fight for an equitable society for people who look like me, which must include a justice system that values the lives of black people (even black criminals) as much as they do white people and criminals. They are not anti-police; instead they advocate for police accountability so that we can create a more equitable system. I can support both police and Black Lives Matter because they are not antithetical and should both be working together to create a safer society for all of us. So I reject the assertion that being pro-Black Lives Matter is being anti-police. It is not. This oppositional positioning partially achieved one purpose: muffling the voices of the oppressed.

In this same manner, we must reject the idea that being anti-racist is being anti-white. Because of the connotations of the term "racism," some find it easy to assert that people speaking against it are simultaneously speaking against white people. We are instead speaking to toxic whiteness and the people who allow its damaging effects to go unchecked.

Push back against white supremacy and the people who knowingly or unknowingly perpetuate it. Once we develop a more thorough understanding of racism and have rid ourselves of the idea that it is only perpetuated by extremists, it is important that you call it out when you see it. For example, I am a member of an online liberal group that I absolutely adore. It is my happy spot where I feel I can openly share my experiences, show every aspect of my personality, and discuss my experiences as a black woman with women who are looking hard at their own whiteness. Although this group is filled with kind, amazing, good women, we occasionally must address instances when someone reveals their unintentional biases and makes problematic statements.

In this group, I have a friend named Gina who, when she sees these type of statements, will begin her response with "I'm going to push back a bit," and then proceed to explain why it is problematic from her position as an anti-racist. She does not attempt to speak FOR people of color; she knows that we have our own voices and can use them well to explain. Yet, she also understands that we get tired of having to do this over and over again, so she speaks to what she has learned about her whiteness as it relates to that particular subject. Each and every time, I am happy that she shows up, not presumptively or condescendingly, but kindly and firmly.

Being anti-racist means making sure that your friends of color are relieved when you show up because you ease the burden they must carry to justify their existence and experience. You should be the person who brings them relief because they know that you have made every effort to understand and to share in the task of getting other folks together on the issue of our humanity. I know that whenever Gina shows up, her statements will not cause further harm. They will be filled with contextual information that many people are often missing, and her ultimate message will be, "I was there once, but here's what I have learned." More than that, she requires none of her friends of color to do the emotional labor for her in the process. She does the heavy-lifting herself and creates additional white allies in the process.

Be like Gina.

Confront racist notions where they live. You do not become anti-racist while performing community service in predominantly black neighborhoods. Your work as an anti-racist must be done in the institutions, neighborhoods, organizations, and systems where racist notions are incubated. Speaking to members of minority groups allows you to develop a better understanding of their experiences and aids you in breaking down your own conscious and unconscious biases, something that is necessary as you develop your anti-racism tool box. However, you must take what you have learned back to your coworker who constantly spouts discriminatory views of people of color or your church that is not very inclusive and continues to lose minority congregants. You must speak up in the PTA meetings and city council meetings. Otherwise, the work you do in the "hood" is simply placing a bandaid over a bullet wound.

Continuously learn. For every step you take, you should be learning all you can so that you can move to the next step and the one after that. If ever you get to a point where you think you've read it all, learned it all, or understand it all, you should probably turn back and start again at step one. We just cannot possibly learn everything, but we can do our best to be open to education on any subject. At the end of this book, I have included a list of 365 people, events, civilizations, etc., that I am asking you to research, one a day for a year. I cannot even begin to express to you how much I learned as I researched for it. My friends Ken and Amy joined me in searching for items for this list, and both agreed that there was so much that we wanted to learn more about. Creating this list reinforced this important concept for me: for as much as I know about a variety of subjects, there is an infinite amount of knowledge out there for me to discover.

Be intentional in discussing race and discrimination with our children, family, and friends. Use your knowledge and courage to create more allies. Race is something that I must confront and discuss every day, not just because of the nature of my business, but because of my skin color. When I was still in the classroom, I removed the stigma of discussing race by talking about it every day. Some discussions were formal, such as when we discussed the nuances and contextuality of the use of the "n" word in August Wilson's *Fences*. Others were very informal, mentioned in passing or normalized as a part of my experience. Often, I would add a question to assignments about literature and writing that asked students to consider an idea through a cultural lens.

Whatever I accomplish with this book, I hope you are at least left with the understanding and mandate that you MUST discuss race. On purpose. When incidents occur. When you are learning something new. When you are parenting. When you are making major decisions, especially if they may impact minorities within your community. It is not enough for you to accidentally trip and end up in a discussion about race. Instead, you should set your moral GPS so that it steers you directly to these important and necessary conversations.

Stand up for black children. We need only look at statistics to discover why black children need more people standing up for them. Black and brown children are punished at a rate disproportionate to their white counterparts, beginning as early as kindergarten. Young black girls are viewed as less innocent than white children beginning as early as five years of age (Shapiro, "Study: Black Girls..."). Black children are less likely to receive trauma-informed care despite bearing the weight of both personal trauma as well as racial trauma.

When Marvel's *Black Panther* came out, one of the aspects of the movie that I was impressed with (and there were many) was the complexity of the villain Killmonger. As an English teacher, I taught about antagonists and protagonists and had previously used Graham Greene's "The Destructors" to teach about anti-heroes. However, Killmonger far surpassed previous examples I had used. He was a villain of King T'Chaka's own creation; his anger appeared justified though we could disagree with his methods. His fate, though necessary, saddened us.

Around this time, an African proverb began circulating that really brought it all home. "The child who is not embraced by the village will burn it down to feel its warmth." I often wonder how many black children we set on a negative pathway because of our failure to protect them. How many children have we judged as criminal when it is our failure to embrace and support that have contributed to their outcomes?

You have the power to provide support according to whatever resources you have. If you can support financially, donate to programs that benefit black children. When you can, speak to someone in your network and help provide an opportunity. If you see an injustice, take action as aggressively as you would if it were your own child.

In the black community especially (although it is found in other cultures and communities), we practice what anthropologists call fictive kinship. This is basically when one chooses to accept an individual as a member of your family when you have no blood or marital kinship ties. My extended family has occasionally joked about the number of cousins, aunties, uncles, and sisters I claim as mine, but I would not change that aspect of my personality for anything in the world. The assigning of a kinship role indicates a commitment to maintain relationship that is deeper than what one would find with friends or acquaintances.

I am asking you all to do the same with black children. Do not just think of them as someone else's child. Consider them as your own, whether they become your son, daughter, niece, nephew, or grandchild. Whatever intervention and advocacy looks like for your actual child is exactly what it should look like for children of color. If you wouldn't accept it for your own, you should not be willing to accept it for black children, either. Anti-racism requires that we stand up for children of color in our schools, systems, and societies so that we plant seeds of acceptance, not rejection.

Do not hide behind whiteness when it is convenient. Remember that your black counterparts do not have the luxury of retreating when faced with racial hatred, microaggressions, or racial stress. If you are to be anti-racist, you must be brave. You cannot use your whiteness as a shield to protect you when it becomes hard to deal with racism and discrimination. As Jon Stewart once said, "You're tired of hearing about it? Imagine how f*cking exhausting it is living it."

Let go of resources that are being hoarded in your neighborhoods, schools, and institutions. According to EdBuild, a nonprofit that addresses school funding disparities, predominantly white school districts receive $23 billion more in funding per year than predominantly minority districts. Students in impoverished, predominantly nonwhite districts receive approximately $1300 less per student than the national average, while students in predominantly white impoverished districts receive about $130 less. Because of racist policies, economic, social, and service resources are being hoarded in white communities while non-white citizens are left to fend for themselves. As a non-racist, you must be willing to advocate for the equalization of these resources. You must seek to ensure that children in poor nonwhite districts have equal access to technology, educational resources, and supplies. This is sometimes hard for people to do because the loss of privilege can feel like oppression. The loss of money can feel like you are being robbed, but you must look at it for the opportunity that it can provide.

Consider this. Over the last few years, Amazon has been actively searching for a place to build their headquarters. My city, St. Louis, put in a bid, but was rejected and lost the opportunity to add thousands of jobs to the region. Part of the reason was because they looked at our schools and felt that the St. Louis region as a whole could not guarantee a skilled and educated workforce. Basically, our racist policies cost us quite a bit of money in terms of tax revenue, area GDP, etc.

In 2017, a Chicago nonprofit called the Metropolitan Planning Council paired with the Urban Institute, a Washington-based organization, to release a report on the impact of segregation in the Chicago area. For it, researchers "analyzed segregation patterns in the 100 largest metropolitan areas in the country and found that if Chicago — the fifth most racially and economically segregated city in the country — were to lower its level of segregation to the national median of those 100 cities, it would have a profound impact on the entire Chicago region, including raising the region's gross domestic product, raising incomes and lowering the homicide rate" (Chiles, "Everyone Pays a Hefty Price..."). Basically, decreasing segregation (and therefore, the hoarding of resources) would have increased regional earnings by $4.4 billion, increased the region's GDP by $8 billion, and decreased the number of homicides in 2016 by 229 people.

My city is at least as segregated as the Chicago area, if not more. We are comprised by a number of townships, and we have the unique distinction of having a surrounding county that is governed and operated separately from our inner city. This was done in the mid-1800s for the purpose of retaining resources into small townships, some of which became sundown towns (cities where African Americans were told to "not let the sun go down" on their backs). Anti-racists must actively petition for a release of resources to communities where they've previously been denied.

Vote for political candidates who support policies that benefit all demographic groups. Call those politicians and hold them accountable for implementing change. We are currently existing in a political atmosphere where there are politicians who are openly hostile to racial and religious minorities. Some people vote for these individuals because they genuinely agree with them, but others support them because of party affiliation or because that candidate supports one particular issue. However, someone with an anti-racist mentality realizes that even their vote is essential to fighting systemic racism. As I have previously stated, racist ideas come from racist policies. Racist policies come from politicians whose central focus is on other concerns than their most vulnerable constituents.

I will not tell you a party to vote for because voting is a sacred privilege. If it were not, efforts to disenfranchise certain groups of people would not have been so egregious throughout American history. What I will ask is that you make your vote a conscious act of solidarity with the most vulnerable in our country. Understand the full impact of the policies you are voting for and research the individuals who are asking to represent you. Make sure they do not just represent some of us, but ALL of us, instead. Vote for the policies and politicians that will benefit the most people in our country.

Support the economic development of minority businesses and communities. Since I began my business, I have been overwhelmed to discover the number of black entrepreneurs and black-owned businesses there are out there. Many people are working very hard to build their businesses so that they can improve their communities and give back to those in need. Our support helps them achieve that goal, as well as helps build generational wealth for African American families, something that our country's policies has often prevented people in minority neighborhoods from doing (see the GI Bill, the origins of unemployment insurance, etc.).

Practice self-care and support your friends of color in their need for self-care, as well. One of my favorite sayings about self-care is this: you cannot pour from an empty cup. What fills you back up so you can be ready to continue the fight the next day? It is important that you regularly tend to your inner self. While anti-racism calls for you to engage with race and discrimination regularly, it is exhausting to do so, which means that you have to recharge just as regularly. While you're at it, take your friends of color and anti-racist white allies with you. One of the ways that I regularly recharge is by spending time doing something I enjoy with friends who do not require emotional labor from me. This could be going to dinner, having a movie night, sitting in the garage of my March sister's commercial building and hanging out, going on a "staycation" with my girlfriends, having a spa day, etc. Self-care looks differently for everyone, but it should achieve the goal of helping you refocus on your purpose and recharge your socioemotional battery.

As you dive deeper into the work of anti-racism, you will find that it is easier and easier to differentiate between being non-racist and anti-racist. Your ultimate purpose should always be effectuating as much change as possible so that people of color have equal access to our society.

I believe in you.

You can do it.

I'm depending on you.

ACKNOWLEDGEMENTS

In Africa, there is an ancient proverb that states, "I am because we are." I often refer to this beautiful concept in my mind as I think about my process of becoming. I am because of all the beautiful people God placed in my life. I have been richly blessed with a mosaic of people who have left little gifts within me and encouraged me to share them with others.

My journey began with parents who were models for learning, no matter how untraditional the path. They also taught me so much about the rewards of caring for others, no matter how difficult that may be. I am forever grateful to my mother, Sandra Saunders, and my dad, Lonnie Grimes, Jr., for being the best people that I know or will ever meet. Although they divorced almost 30 years ago, their weekly lunches show me everything I need to know about love, friendship, forgiveness, intelligence, compassion, thoughtfulness, and joy. They've shown me that when everything else falls away, friendship and love will always win the day.

In the end, an imperfect marriage led to a perfect friendship and two extremely blessed and cherished daughters. My sister and I are the best of friends, and we came to that because of my parents' example. There is nothing in this world that I cannot do in my sister's eyes, and she is honestly my hero. Through her, I have my brother-in-law, my nieces Erika and Savannah, and my nephews Chase and Devin.

Through my dad's second marriage, we were blessed with LG, who really made our family complete. Sometimes, when we are with others who aren't familiar with how our family works, we confuse them. There are so many questions that people have about how all of this blended family works. Just know that it does. Mom, Dad, Staci, Shann, Erika, Chase, Savannah, Devin, LG, Jimmel, Jordan, Jalen, Rion, Kennedy, Sergio, and me. That's our family. No matter what.

Others that I must acknowledge for their role in my life, my work, and my development:

Ray H. Waters--I've listened and I've heard.. Thank you for investing so much time and love into me. I know that I am because you are because Willie Mae was.

Gregory D. Tharpe--You're my best friend. Unc, a day doesn't go by that I don't know how much you love and believe in me. Here's to our forever friendship, our training and barbecue business, and the day when you "quit me" to start your own empire. (wink)

Fortune Russell--Second moms don't come any better than you. Thank you for always listening and loving.

Mary Ann Blair--For being the most compact, beautiful package of pure love in the world. I can't imagine having a better mother-in-law than you, Mama, and I certainly appreciate how blessed I am with you. Thank you for loving me, no matter comes our way.

Barbara J. Mikel--You're the best best friend a girl could ever have. Thank you for being your best you and, as a result, making me a better me.

My little brother Jamon and my little sisters Herbia and Maria, i love you so very much. I'm incredibly blessed to be your big sister.

Candra K. Gill--I have never, and will never, forget everything you taught me and all the belief you had in me. Twenty-plus years later, I am still grateful and strive to not let you down.

Maggie Huffman--Thank you for every time you asked, "So, when are you writing your book?," every time you volunteered me for something, and every time you showed up for me. You're my wonderwall.

Tristian Townes--My angel. "Now cracks a noble heart--goodnight, sweet Prince, and flights of angels sing thee to thy rest" (Hamlet V.2.258-259) You are missed every day, cousin. #TrusttheProcess

Dana Parker--You already know. Thank you for dreaming bigger for me than I could for myself.

Erin Armknecht--Thanks for starting as my editor and becoming my motivator, my audience, and my friend.

Erin Brennan--Thanks for the joke that turned into my title.

Pastor Steve and Lady Rita Smith--Thank you for always loving me as family, from the very moment I met you, and for letting "your light so shine before men that they may see your good works and glorify your Father who is in heaven."--Matthew 5:16

Marquita Blair-Pettiford--You are more than my sister-in-law; you are my friend and my star. You are truly majestic.

I also want to shout out for a few people for being inspirations and supports for me: Nadida Amatullah-Matin, Dana Kelly, all of my St. Louis Women's March sisters, Neva Sprung, Mike Hazelton (my Sunshine), Patricia Sims, Joy Bryant, David Kirkman, Rebecca Langrall, Trever Toll, Sarah Shavers, Ken Susman and Amy Miller (thank you both for all your help with the "365 Days of Learning" list), Lindsey Keirsey (I so appreciate your help with my Recommended Reading List), and all my family and friends.

I especially want to thank my wonderful husband, who has been nothing but supportive through every dream I've had. When I wanted to start my own company and non-profit, he said do it. When I wanted to dedicate myself to it full time, he worked harder to make sure I didn't have to worry about the financials. When I said I was writing a book, he did whatever he could to make sure I had time and space to write. Thank you, honey, for believing in me. God made you just for me, and I love you with all that I am.

Important Terms to Know

Below, I have listed and defined several terms that are important to know as you begin discussing and researching further. Please note that some of these terms are also listed in my "365 of Learning" list. The reason for the duplication is simple: here, I have given you a basic definition, while through that list, I am asking you to think about it deeply, search for examples, and ask extension questions to be sure you have a clear understanding of its meaning and can thoughtfully explain it to others.

anti-racism: the position a person takes when their primary focus is to deconstruct the systems that create racist policies and the racist ideas that are generated as a result.

appropriation: taking aspects of a culture without crediting that culture or, more subtly, the taking of aspects of a culture while the people of that culture continue to experience discrimination for engaging in that portion of their culture. i.e. cornrows being renamed "boxer braids" and credited as a trend started by Kim Kardashian (a white reality star) while the military and employers discriminate against black people for wearing braids.

assimilation: the expectation that a group of people gain acceptance through the adoption of the cultural norms and practices of the dominant culture, while rejecting their own culture.

code-switching: the skill of being capable of alternating between two languages or the norms of two separate cultures.

emotional labor: managing your feelings in order to meet organizational, social, or societal demands for acceptance, safety, or success.

inclusion: the state of being accepted and empowered within an organization or group.

integration: the combining of people together with the goal being equity.

intersectionality: the place where a group's separate identities join to create characteristics and issues that are unique to that group.

justice: the application of fairness and moral rightness.

microaggression: subtle or indirect discrimination, whether intentional or unintentional, against members of a marginalized group.

racism: prejudice plus power; the belief that one race is superior to another combined the power to impact the socioeconomic condition of the race as a result.

> **individual racism:** the beliefs and actions of an individual which perpetuates the racist ideas generated from racist policies
> **systemic racism:** the implementation of policies, programs, and laws that negatively impact the ability of one or more races to fully access their rights and meet with societal justice
> **internalized racism:** acceptance of the racist ideas the majority race has against marginalized

groups by members of that group, resulting in a person valuing the majority culture and perceived characteristics over one's own

segregation: setting people or groups apart because of perceived differences. Intentional isolation.

systemic change: fundamental change within a system that impacts each part, including other systems that are connected.

white fragility: defensiveness or anger experienced by a white person in the face of racial stress.

365 Days of Learning

Because I hope you will be open and engaged in continual learning, I am providing you with a list of important terms, people, and events to research in your first year. When you are done reading this book, please browse this list. If there are any terms you feel knowledgeable enough about to teach to others, please highlight them. After that, I ask you to look up the terms that are not highlighted using credible websites so that you can learn more about them.

Please note that these items have not been placed in any particular order. I have randomized them in order to equalize their importance and significance to understanding the totality of the minority experience a bit better. They include important people, events, vocabulary, poetry, songs, and essays. I have listed important books on a separate list. Though most of the subjects are related to the African-American experience, I have also tried to include people and events from other experiences, as well.

As you research each day, see if you use all of the question stems in the questions that you answer:

- What?
    - What happened?
    - What caused it?
    - What were the results?
    - What can we learn from this?
    - What can we do to stop/change it?

- What internal struggles might this person/character face?

- Who?
  - Who was involved?
  - Who helped/hindered?
  - Who benefited/was negatively impacted?

- Where?
  - Where did the main events take place?
  - Where were the people involved from?
  - Where (in what areas) were people impacted?
  - Where do we see remnants of this in today's society?

- Why?
  - Why did it happen?
  - Why did people respond negatively/positively?
  - Why did change happen?
  - Why was this implemented?
  - Why has this person/event/poem/art continued to be relevant?
  - Why hasn't this been widely taught?

- How?
  - How was this significant?
  - How were others impacted?
  - How did society/people/policy change as a result?
  - How have we continued to be impacted?

Learning about each item listed is the first step. Considering how it fits into the bigger picture is the point. So, please be sure to read, remember, reflect, and reconsider each day from a thoughtful, honest place.

DAY	TERM TO RESEARCH
1	the difference between diversity and inclusion
2	institutional racism
3	internalized oppression/racism
4	intersectionality
5	implicit bias
6	Jim Crow laws
7	Plessy v. Ferguson
8	redlining
9	sun down towns
10	Phyllis Wheatley
11	Thomas Jefferson's response to Phyllis Wheatley
12	the 3/5 Compromise
13	environmental racism
14	anti-racism
15	Ida B. Wells
16	the treatment of black women in the suffragist movement.
17	microaggressions
18	The Southern Strategy
19	Lee Atwater and coded language
20	the trope of the "welfare queen"
21	Juneteenth
22	colonialism
23	segregation
24	assimilation
25	The Green Book (not the movie; the actual

	historic book)
26	disenfranchisement
27	the "one drop" rule
28	the origins of jazz
29	Maxine Waters
30	Fair Housing Act
31	Cora I. Parchment and Georgia Ann Robinson
32	colorism and the "paper bag" test
33	the significance of spirit animals in Native American culture
34	James Baldwin's "A Letter to My Nephew"
36	Native American Civilizations prior to 1492
37	the mythology of "reverse racism"
38	Kansas City Monarchs
39	the politicization of black hair
40	Anansi the Spider
41	Scottsboro trial
42	Enheduanna
43	Josephine Baker
44	The Red Summer of 1919
45	Claude McKay's "If We Must Die" and its significance
46	the history of the "40 acres and a mule" concept
47	the Wilmington Insurrection
48	the East St. Louis race riots of 1917
49	Pruitt Igoe
50	Axum Empire
51	National Association for the Advancement of Colored People (NAACP)
52	Fannie Lou Hamer

53	minstrel shows and blackface
54	*The Birth of a Nation*
55	The Kingdom of Ghana
56	"We Wear the Mask" by Paul Laurence Dunbar
57	The Great Migration
58	Muraski Shikibu
59	tone policing
60	What happened during school desegregation?
61	Amy Hunter's TED-X talk "Lucky Zip Codes"
62	The Solid South
63	70s blaxploitation films
64	Central Park Five
65	Brown v. Board of Education
66	Harry F. Byrd, Sr. and massive resistance strategy
67	Christine Jorgensen
68	Michael Brown, Jr.
69	the origin of blues
70	Amelia Boynton-Robinson
71	Satchel Paige
72	misogynoir
73	white privilege
74	Nat Turner
75	Alfred Masters
76	Selena
77	the impact of the War on Drugs in the black community
78	Defense of Marriage Act
79	Sandra Bland

80	Standing Rock protests
81	Sylvia Rivera
82	reproductive exploitation of African Americans
83	Elijah McCoy
84	The Tulsa Race Riots and Black Wall Street
85	James Weldon Johnson's "Fifty Years"
86	Ryan Coogler
87	Legacy Admission policies v. affirmative action
88	Little Rock Nine
89	code-switching
90	Japanese internment camps during World War 2
91	Jimi Hendrix
92	Dorothy Height
93	phrenology
94	the trope of the absent black father
95	Red Cloud
96	Thurgood Marshall
97	Big Mama Thornton
98	Ruby Bridges
99	Peggy McIntosh's "Unpacking the Invisible Knapsack"
100	The Zulu Empire
101	Charles Hamilton Houston
102	"white flight"
103	the Great Library of Alexandria
104	Abdul-Wakil M. Kamal
105	Congo Square (New Orleans)
106	Black Elk
107	white feminism

108	Onesimus
109	Native American civilizations prior to colonialism
110	the real "Betty Boop"--Esther Jones
111	Henrietta Lacks
112	Sharice Davids
113	Kwanzaa
114	the Battle of Hayes Pond
115	racist intent of IQ tests
116	Septima Poinsette Clark
117	ethnocentrism
118	Black Hawk
119	school-to-prison pipeline
120	"super predators"
121	Bayard Rustin
122	the "angry black woman" trope
123	Huma Abedin
124	The Tuskegee experiments
125	Black cowboys in the American West
126	Ancient Carthage
127	Carter G. Woodson
128	The Navajo Code Talkers
129	Afro Latinx erasure
130	anti-miscegenation laws
131	Loving v. Virginia
132	Alexander Twilight
133	the achievement gap
134	Rita Pierson's TED talk "Every Kid Needs a Champion"

135	Dolores Huerta
136	Spike Lee
137	The ancient city of Kahun
138	Haitian Revolution
139	Grace Hopper
140	the impact of George Washington Carver's peanut experiments on farming in the South. (He did more than invent peanut butter.)
141	Betty Mae Tiger Jumper
142	Nubian Empire
143	The Miami people
144	*Freedom's Journal* newspaper
145	James Marion Sims' gynecological experiments on enslaved black women
146	Lawrence v. Texas
147	Immigration Acts of 1907, 1917, 1921, and 1924
148	Dr. Joycelyn Elders
149	Huey P. Newton
150	Watch Ava DuVernay's 13th
151	the historical Pocahontas
152	The Civil Rights Act of 1964
153	Ronald McNair
154	Fletcher Henderson
155	N. Scott Momaday's "The Delight Song of Tsoai-talee"
156	Bull Connor
157	Alberta Williams King
158	Houston Riot of 1917
159	James McCune Smith
160	Langston Hughes's "Theme for English B"

161	The Songhai Empire
162	Shirley Chisholm
163	Robert Johnson
164	Emmett Till
165	Shelley v. Kraemer
166	BB King
167	BlackLivesMatter.com--What We Believe
168	Sitting Bull
169	Nefertiti
170	school funding in predominantly white v. predominantly black school districts
171	Marie Curie
172	Nina Simone's "Four Women"
173	mathematics in Ancient Africa
174	Claudette Colvin
175	The Incan Empire
176	Ashmun Institute
177	Sarah Jane Woodson Early
178	Muhammad Ali
179	Nelson Mandela
180	The Lakota People
181	the Labyrinth at Hawara
182	Asa Phillip Randolph
183	The University at Timbuktu
184	Marie Maynard Daly
185	the impact of the "three strikes" policy and mandatory minimum sentencing
186	Curt Flood
187	Stonewall Riots

188	Marsha P. Johnson
189	Bill Russell
190	The Modoc War (1872 to 1873)
191	Frankie Muse Freeman
192	Selma and Dr. Martin Luther King, Jr.
193	The official language of the United States
194	Stokely Carmichael
195	Read "David Walker" by Rita Dove
196	the unequal access to Stand Your Ground laws
197	Kofi Annan
198	Chuck Berry
199	Nella Larsen
200	The Mali Empire
201	Wilberforce University
202	Martin R. Delany
203	Kimberly M. Blaeser
204	Bobby Seales
205	Don't Ask, Don't Tell policy
206	Wounded Knee
207	Rebecca Davis Lee Crumpler
208	Mae C. Jemison
209	Octavia Butler
210	Eric Garner
211	Daisy Bates
212	Bureau of Indian Affairs Takeover (1972)
213	Laura Wheeling Waring
214	Gullah Geechee culture
215	Sequoyah
216	Edward Alexander Bouchet

217	Ella Baker
218	Karen Uhlenbeck
219	Mansa Musa I
220	Dr. Martin Luther King's "Eulogy for the Martyred Children" (read full manuscript)
221	Maurice Ashley
222	Lois Mailou Jones
223	Read "Revolt of the Evil Fairies" by Ted Poston
224	Tommie Smith and John Carlos
225	Sam Cooke
226	The ancient city of Amarna
227	Misty Copeland
228	Amiri Baraka
229	poll taxes
230	Percy Julian
231	Soul City, North Carolina and Floyd McKissick
232	Maya Angelou's "On the Pulse of Morning"
233	Sophia Danenberg
234	Watts Riots
235	The Trail of Tears
236	The Mayan Empire
237	The Benin Empire
238	Francois-Dominique Toussaint Louverture
239	Rashida Tlaib
240	Shane Koyczan's "To This Day..."
241	Dr. Ruth Simmons
242	gentrification
243	Moses Fleetwood Walker
244	the Sandia Indians (Native Americans)

245	the Land of Punt
246	Nikki Giovanni's "Nikki-Rosa"
247	Pele
248	Amina of the Hausa
249	the 10 Point Plan of the Black Panther Party
250	Paul Robeson
251	Sammu-Ramat
252	James Van Der Zee
253	Marian Anderson
254	Trayvon Martin
255	the pyramids of Sudan
256	Grandfather Clause
257	Dr. M. L. King's "The Casualties of the War in Vietnam"
258	Lucy Hicks Anderson
259	L. A. Riots and Rodney King
260	Alpha Phi Alpha
261	Mike Carey
262	Buffalo Soldiers
263	Gwendolyn Brooks's "We Real Cool" and "Sadie and Maud"
264	the Kingdom of Monomotapa
265	Miriam Makeba
266	Ruth E. Carter and the cultural significance of the costumes in *Black Panther*, the movie
267	Chimamanda Ngozi Adichie's TED talk "The Danger of the Single Story"
268	Emperor Lalibela of Ethiopia
269	Nannie Helen Burroughs
270	Roger Taney's Supreme Court opinion in the

	Dred Scott v. John F. A. Sanford case
271	The Ferguson Report--Department of Justice
272	Forward Through Ferguson
273	Ilhan Omar
274	Anna Arnold Hedgeman
275	Barack Obama's Speech on Race 2008
276	Nong Toom
277	Motown
278	Samuel J. Battle
279	Sam Cooke's "A Change is Gonna Come"
280	Stagecoach Mary Fields
281	Aisha (Muhammad's wife)
282	Matthew Henson
283	The Solid South
284	Alpha Kappa Alpha
285	Dr. M. L. King's "I've Been to the Mountaintop" speech
286	Emilie du Chatelet
287	Tamir Rice
288	The Grand Mosque of Djenne`
289	Sandra Cisneros's "Those Who Don't" from *The House on Mango Street*
290	Hiram Revels
291	Omega Psi Phi
292	Marian Anderson
293	Delta Sigma Theta
294	the GI bill and the exclusion of black soldiers
295	Bishop Desmond Tutu
296	The Atlanta Race Riot of 1906

297	gerrymandering
298	Melody Hobson's TED talk "Color Blind or Color Brave"
299	Rosewood
300	Kappa Alpha Psi
301	Alvin Ailey
302	Tzu-hsi of China
303	W. E. B. DuBois
304	Sidney Poitier
305	tokenism
306	The Iroquois Nation
307	Pauli Murray
308	Kingdom of Lunda
309	Sigma Gamma Rho
310	"Strange Fruit" by Billie Holiday
311	Shirley Ann Jackson
312	Jordan Davis
313	Lucy McBath
314	Phi Beta Sigma/Zeta Phi Beta
315	Joan Higginbotham
316	The Mayan Civilization
317	Aretha Franklin
318	Mary McLeod Bethune
319	James Weldon Johnson's "Lift Ev'ry Voice and Sing"
320	Jupiter Hammon
321	The Second Wounded Knee (1973)
322	Zora Neale Hurston
323	the 13th Amendment

324	convict leasing
325	Iota Phi Theta
326	Frazier B. Baker
327	Hank Aaron
328	"Incident" by Countee Cullen
329	Mary Jones (1784-1864)
330	Cesar Chavez
331	Jessie Fauset
332	Katherine Johnson
333	The Nok Civilization
334	Mother Bethel A.M.E. Church
335	The Detroit Race Riot of 1943
336	James "Cool Papa" Bell
337	Fulani People
338	Paul Laurence Dunbar's "Sympathy"
339	Fred Begay
340	Pharaoh Hatshepsut
341	Obergefell v. Hodges
342	Philando Castile
343	The Yoruba People
344	Venus and Serena Williams
345	cultural appropriation
346	The Taino
347	Thomas L. Jennings
348	Read "The Kind of Light that Shines on Texas" by Reginald McKnight
349	Indian Wars
350	Olaudah Equiano
351	the concept of the "magical Negro"

352	white savior trope in literature and film
353	Angela Morley
354	The Aztec Civilization
355	Dick Gregory
356	Stevie Wonder's "Happy Birthday"
357	The Kingdom of Kush
358	Maroons (people)
359	Maria Tallchief
360	Simon Bolivar
361	Gwendolyn Bennett
362	Mary Seacole
363	Toni Morrison
364	Husuni Kubwa
365	Langston Hughes' "I, Too"

Suggested Reading List
So Many books, so Little time!

The books listed below are ones that are required reading as we move toward equity in our society. Though the majority of the books are for all people, a few are written specifically for people in the educational field, and I have labeled them accordingly. They are listed in alphabetical order, not in order of importance. Wherever you choose to start is up to you, as long as you learn a little bit more each day. Enjoy!

For Everyone

Alexander, Michelle. *The New Jim Crow: Mass Incarceration in the Age of Colorblindness*. Samuel DeWitt Proctor Conference, 2011.

Anderson, Carol. *White Rage the Unspoken Truth of Our Racial Divide*. Bloomsbury, an Imprint of Bloomsbury Publishing Plc, 2017.

Angelou, Maya. "*I Know Why the Caged Bird Sings*". Penguin, 2008.

Asim, Jabari. *We Can't Breathe on Black Lives, White Lies, and the Art of Survival*. Picador, 2018.

Baldwin, James. *Go Tell It on the Mountain: The Fire Next Time: If Beale Street Could Talk*. Black Expressions Book Club, 2004.

Banaji, Mahzarin R., and Anthony G. Greenwald. *Blindspot Hidden Biases of Good People*. Delacorte Press, 2013.

Brown, Austin Channing. *I'm Still Here: Black Dignity in a World Made for Whiteness*. Convergent Books, 2018.

Brown, Dee. *Bury My Heart at Wounded Knee: an Indian History of the American West*. Fall River Press, 2014.

Carter, Forrest, and Rennard Strickland. *The Education of Little Tree*. University of New Mexico Press, 2008.

Cisneros, Sandra. *The House on Mango Street*. McGraw-Hill College, 2000.

Coates, Ta-Nehisi, and Klaus Amann. *Between the World and Me*. Reclam, 2017.

Coates, Ta-Nehisi. *We Were Eight Years in Power: a Journey Through the Obama Era*. Random House Inc, 2017.

Cooper, Brittney. *Eloquent Rage: a Black Feminist Discovers Her Superpower*. Picador, 2019.

Douglass, Frederick. *Narrative of the Life of Frederick Douglass: an American Slave*. Digireads.com Pub., 2016.

Dunbar-Ortiz, Roxanne. *An Indigenous Peoples' History of the United States*. Beacon Press, 2015.

Eddo-Lodge, Reni. *Why I'm No Longer Talking to White People about Race*. Bloomsbury Circus, 2017.

Gates, Henry Louis, and Nellie Y. McKay. *The Norton Anthology of African American Literature*. W.W. Norton & Co., 2004.

Griffin, Christi M. *Incarcerations in Black and White: the Subjugation of Black America*. C. Griffin Publishing, 2013.

Gyasi, Yaa. *Homegoing*. Penguin Books Ltd., 2017.

Hosseini, Khaled. A *Thousand Splendid Suns*. W. Ross MacDonald School Resource Services Library, 2011.

Hurston, Zora Neale. *Their Eyes Were Watching God*. HarperLuxe, 2008.

Jerkins, Morgan. *This Will Be My Undoing: Living at the Intersection of Black, Female, and Feminist in (White) America*. Harper Perennial, 2018.

Jones, Tayari. *American Marriage: a Novel*. Harper Collins Canada, 2019.

Katznelson, Ira. *When Affirmative Action Was White*. W.W. Norton, 2005.

Kendi, Ibram X. *Stamped from the Beginning the Definitive History of Racist Ideas in America*. The Bodley Head, 2017.

Khan-Cullors, Patrisse, et al. *When They Call You a Terrorist: a Black Lives Matter Memoir*. Canongate, 2019.

Kidd, Sue Monk. *The Invention of Wings*. Double Day Large Print, 2014.

Laymon, Kiese. *Heavy: an American Memoir*. Simon & Schuster, 2018.

Leary, Joy DeGruy. *Post Traumatic Slave Syndrome: America's Legacy of Enduring Injury and Healing*. Joy DeGruy Publications, 2017.

Lewis, Earl, and Nancy Cantor. *Our Compelling Interests: the Value of Diversity for Democracy and a Prosperous Society*. Princeton University Press, 2017.

Mah, Adeline Yen. *Chinese Cinderella: the Secret Story of an Unwanted Daughter*. Royal New Zealand Foundation of the Blind, 2011.

Morrison, Toni. *The Bluest Eye*. Vintage, 2016.

Nerburn, Kent. *The Wisdom of the Native Americans*. New World Library, 1999.

Obama, Barack. *Dreams from My Father: a Story of Race and Inheritance*. Canongate, 2004.

Obama, Michelle. *Becoming*. Crown, an Imprint of the Crown Publishing Group, 2018.

Orange, Tommy. THERE THERE. Random House Large Print Publishing, 2018.

Rankine, Claudia. *Citizen: an American Lyric*. Penguin Books, 2015.

Skloot, Rebecca. *The Immortal Life of Henrietta Lacks Book Club in a Bag*. Broadway Paperbacks, 2011.

Stevenson, Bryan. JUST MERCY. Spiegel & Grau, 2015.

Stone, Nic. *Odd One Out*. Random House Children's Books, 2018.

Tatum, Beverly Daniel. *Can We Talk about Race?: and Other Conversations in an Era of School Resegregation*. Beacon, 2008.

Thomas, Angie, et al. *The Hate u Give*. Moon Young Adult, 2017.

Thompson-Spires, Nafissa. *Heads of the Colored People*. Vintage,, 2019.

Walker, Alice. *The Color Purple*. Harcourt, 2003.

Whitehead, Colson. *The Underground Railroad: a Novel*. Anchor Books, a Division of Penguin Random House LLC, 2018.

Wilkerson, Isabel. *The Warmth of Other Suns*. Random House, 2010.

Wise, Tim J. *White like Me: Reflections on Race from a Privileged Son: the Remix*. Soft Skull Press, 2011.

Wright, Richard. *Black Boy: a Record of Childhood and Youth*. Harper Perennial, 2007.

Uchida, Yoshiko. *Picture Bride A Novel*. Paw Prints, 2008.

X, Malcolm, et al. *The Autobiography of Malcolm X*. Ballantine Books, 1992.

Zoboi, Ibi Aanu, and Jane Austen. *Pride*. Balzer   Bray, an Imprint of HarperCollins Publishers, 2018.

FOR EDUCATORS

Bolgatz, Jane. *Talking Race in the Classroom*. Teachers College Press, 2005.

Delpit, Lisa. "*Multiplication Is for White People* . New Press, 2014.

Emdin, Christopher. *For White Folks Who Teach in the Hood ... and the Rest of Y'all Too Reality Pedagogy and Urban Education*. Beacon Pr, 2017.

Freire, Paulo, and Myra B. Ramos. *Pedagogy of the Oppressed*. Seabury Press, 1970.

Gay, Geneva. *Culturally Responsive Teaching: Theory, Research, and Practice*. Teachers College Press, 2018.

Howard, Gary R. *We Can't Teach What We Don't Know: White Teachers, Multiracial Schools*. Teachers College Press, 2016.

Moore, Eddie, et al. *The Guide for White Women Who Teach Black Boys: Understanding, Connecting, Respecting*. Corwin, 2018.

Morris, Monique W. *Pushout: the Criminalization of Black Girls in Schools*. New Press, 2018.

Perry, Theresa, et al. *Young, Gifted, and Black Promoting High Achievement among African-American Students*. Beacon Press, 2003.

Pollock, Mica. *Everyday Antiracism Getting Real about Race in School*. New Press, 2008.

Steele, Claude M. *Whistling Vivaldi: How Stereotypes Affect Us and What We Can Do*. W.W. Norton & Company, 2011.

Tatum, Beverly Daniel. *"Why Are All the Black Kids Sitting Together in the Cafeteria?" and Other Conversations about the Development of Racial Identity*. BasicBooks, 1997.

References

Animal Spirit Guides. www.manataka.org/page291.html.

"4 Steps to Process Your Emotions So They Don't Zap Your Energy." *Tiny Buddha*, 24 Mar. 2014, tinybuddha.com/blog/4-steps-process-emotions-dont-zap-energy/.

"A Closer Look at the Demographics of Flint, Michigan." *Fox News*, FOX News Network, www.foxnews.com/us/a-closer-look-at-the-demographics-of-flint-michigan.

Allen, Danielle. "Chapter 2. Toward a Connected Society." *Our Compelling Interests*, 2016, doi:10.1515/9781400881260-006.

Ascd. "Confronting the Racism of Low Expectations." *How Student Progress Monitoring Improves Instruction - Educational Leadership*, www.ascd.org/publications/educational-leadership/nov04/vol62/num03/Confronting-the-Racism-of-Low-Expectations.aspx.

Ascd. "Let's Talk about Racism in Schools." *How Student Progress Monitoring Improves Instruction - Educational Leadership*, www.ascd.org/publications/educational-leadership/nov16/vol74/num03/Let's-Talk-about-Racism-in-Schools.aspx.

Brown Brené. *Daring Greatly: How the Courage to Be Vulnerable Transforms the Way We Live, Love, Parent, and Lead.* Penguin Books Ltd, 2015.

Chiles, Nick. "Everyone Pays A Hefty Price For Segregation, Study Says." NPR, NPR, 31 Mar. 2017, www.npr.org/sections/codeswitch/2017/03/31/522098019/everyone-pays-a-hefty-price-for-segregation-study-says.

Demands, Brenna. "Time to Put Away the Pink Hats, Ladies." *Medium.com*, Medium, 31 Oct. 2018, medium.com/@BrennaDemands/time-to-put-away-the-pink-hats-ladies-4bd9949f17d7.

DiAngelo, Robin. "White Fragility." *The International Journal of Critical Pedagogy*, libjournal.uncg.edu/ijcp/article/view/249.

Fessler, Leah, and Leah Fessler. "An Extremely Clear Definition of Emotional Labor for Anyone Who Still Doesn't Get It." *Quartz at Work*, Quartz, 24 May 2018, qz.com/work/1286996/an-extremely-clear-definition-of-emotional-labor-from-adam-grants-podcast/.

"Flint Water Crisis Fast Facts." CNN, Cable News Network, 6 Dec. 2018, www.cnn.com/2016/03/04/us/flint-water-crisis-fast-facts/index.html.

"Flint, MI." *Data USA*, datausa.io/profile/geo/flint-mi/.

Garcia, Arturo, and Arturo Garcia. "FACT CHECK: Did a U.S. Veteran Influence Kaepernick's 'Take a Knee' Protest of Police Brutality?" *Snopes.com*, www.snopes.com/fact-check/veteran-kaepernick-take-a-knee-anthem/.

"Hate Crime." FBI, FBI, 15 July 2010, ucr.fbi.gov/hate-crime.

Holloway, Kalie and AlterNet. "11 Things White People Can Do to Be Real Anti-Racist Allies." *Alternet,* Alternet.org, 8 Aug. 2016, www.alternet.org/2015/04/11-things-white-peopl e-can-do-be-real-anti-racist-allies/.

"How We Pronounce Student Names, and Why It Matters." *Cult of Pedagogy,* www.cultofpedagogy.com/gift-of-pronunciation/.

"How to Apologize – Asking for Forgiveness Gracefully." *Groupthink - Decision Making Skills Training from MindTools.com,* Mind Tools, www.mindtools.com/pages/article/how-to-apolo gize.htm.

Ingraham, Christopher. "Three Quarters of Whites Don't Have Any Non-White Friends." *The Washington Post,* WP Company, 25 Aug. 2014, www.washingtonpost.com/news/wonk/wp/2014 /08/25/three-quarters-of-whites-dont-have-any -non-white-friends/?utm_term=.bfa8ca719484.

Jones, Robert P. "Self-Segregation: Why It's So Hard for Whites to Understand Ferguson." *The Atlantic,* Atlantic Media Company, 25 Nov. 2014, www.theatlantic.com/national/archive/2014/08/ self-segregation-why-its-hard-for-whites-to-unde rstand-ferguson/378928/.

Jones, Trina, and Kimberly Jade Norwood. "Aggressive Encounters & White Fragility: Deconstructing the Trope of the Angry Black Woman." *Iowa Law Review,* ilr.law.uiowa.edu/print/volume-102-issue-5/aggr essive-encounters-and-white-fragility-deconstruc ting-the-trope-of-the-angry-black-woman/.

"Journey to Freedom." *LinkedIn SlideShare,* 24 June 2009, www.slideshare.net/scottreall/tacoma-pastors-br eakfast.

Kendi, Ibram X. *Stamped from the Beginning the Definitive History of Racist Ideas in America*. The Bodley Head, 2017.

Lewis, Earl, and Nancy Cantor. *Our Compelling Interests: the Value of Diversity for Democracy and a Prosperous Society*. Princeton University Press, 2017.

Lombardo, Clare. "Why White School Districts Have So Much More Money." NPR, NPR, 26 Feb. 2019, www.npr.org/2019/02/26/696794821/why-white -school-districts-have-so-much-more-money?ut m_source=facebook.com&utm_medium=social&ut m_campaign=npr&utm_term=nprnews&utm_cont ent=20190226&fbclid=IwAR3ZUxxpTkwtfjomh1qVv mGcomJUiG_hwBgDZZipqXPTMQIBkjoeRlWcpYE.

McCarthy, Niall. "Report: Number Of Hate Groups in the U.S. Soars to Record High [Infographic]." *Forbes*, Forbes Magazine, 21 Feb. 2019, www.forbes.com/sites/niallmccarthy/2019/02/21 /report-number-of-hate-groups-in-the-u-s-soars -to-record-high-infographic/#10764ef828fa.

Mcintosh, Peggy. "White Privilege and Male Privilege." *Privilege*, pp. 28–40., doi:10.4324/9780429494802-6.

Mitchell, Corey. "Mispronouncing Students' Names: A Slight That Can Cut Deep." *Education Week*, Editorial Project in Education, 20 Feb. 2019, www.edweek.org/ew/articles/2016/05/11/mispr onouncing-students-names-a-slight-that-can.html

NCTSN Admin. "Racial Injustice and Trauma: African Americans in the US: NCTSN Position Statement." *The National Child Traumatic Stress Network*, 1 June 2018, www.nctsn.org/resources/racial-injustice-and-tr auma-african-americans-us-nctsn-position-state ment.

"The Psychology of Prejudice."
UnderstandingPrejudice.org,
secure.understandingprejudice.org/apa/english/p
age10.htm.

"Race in America: Tips on Talking With Children About
Racism." Psychology Today, Sussex Publishers,
www.psychologytoday.com/us/blog/the-race-go
od-health/201708/race-in-america-tips-talking-c
hildren-about-racism.

"Say My Name, Say My Name: Quvenzhané Wallis."
HelloGiggles, HelloGiggles,
hellogiggles.com/reviews-coverage/say-my-name
-say-my-name-quvenzhane-wallis/.

Shapiro, T. Rees. "Study: Black Girls Viewed as 'Less
Innocent' than White Girls." The Washington Post,
WP Company, 27 June 2017,
www.washingtonpost.com/local/education/study
-black-girls-viewed-as-less-innocent-than-white-
girls/2017/06/27/3fbedc32-5ae1-11e7-a9f6-7c329
6387341_story.html?utm_term=.dbee565119fd.

Tatum, Beverly Daniel. Can We Talk about Race?: and
Other Conversations in an Era of School
Resegregation. Beacon, 2008.

Weiss, Debra Cassens. "Firm Uses Minorities as 'Diversity
Props' to Impress Clients, Suit Alleges." ABA Journal,
www.abajournal.com/news/article/law-firm-viola
ted-fraud-laws-by-misrepresenting-inclusiveness-
to-would-be-associates-suit-alleges.

Wong, Gloria, et al. "The What, the Why, and the How: A
Review of Racial Microaggressions Research in
Psychology." Race and Social Problems, vol. 6, no. 2,
2013, pp. 181–200., doi:10.1007/s12552-013-9107-9.

Made in the USA
Monee, IL
02 November 2020